A Breast Cancer Journey

From There to Here

DIANE DAVIES

A Breast Cancer Journey: From There to Here
Copyright © 2023 by Diane Davies

ISBN: Paperback: 978-1959151241
e-book: 978-1959151258

The Reading Glass Books
1-888-420-3050
www.readingglassbooks.com
production@readingglassbooks.com

Contents

Foreword

HOW CAN A diagnosis of breast cancer save a woman's life when the disease itself threatens to take her last breath? When Diane Davies was diagnosed with breast cancer in 2004, she had no idea at the time that a joyful and more meaningful life was even possible after breast cancer. But this transformation of her life didn't come without some life lessons for Diane, lessons that changed both her perspective and her attitude, and ultimately saved her life.

Breast Cancer Saved My Life is an important message when facing all of our remaining days, no matter what our state of health is. We can learn a lot from each of the lessons that Diane shares with us in this heartfelt book.

Diane is a teacher at heart, teaching young children all of her adult life in public school. However the diagnosis of breast cancer became the classroom for her life and she was its ardent student.

I encourage you to consider how Diane's lessons can apply to your challenging situation and how the diagnosis of breast cancer, or any cancer or traumatic experience can be improved by adding prayer, gratitude, perspective, grace, comfort, and peace directly into your daily life.

There is a powerful concept in this book that I don't want you to miss… it's the chapter about her healing chair and how it brought so much peace to Diane. Your choice to explore what peace feels like for you after a diagnosis of breast cancer is a powerful gift that only you can give to yourself and it can save your life as well.

In this place of peace is where we find answers that aren't based in fear. In this place of peace is where we connect with what is best for us and not what is best for the Negative Nellies in our life. In this place of peace is where we can connect with what is truly best for our next step forward. Whether it is a chair, a walk in the park, the special place you like to be when you pray, or a corner in the closet, take the time to make it a daily ritual to go to your special healing place and connect with the peace and safety that lies within each of us. This is a powerful tool to use every day to face the healing journey before you.

Healing after a diagnosis of breast cancer takes patience. Perhaps this is one of the most challenging lessons of all because we feel time is against us when facing breast cancer. Yet the body needs time to heal and our emotions need to have a chance to move out of the darkness of overwhelm and despair and into the light of hope and possibilities. Diane addresses the lesson of patience as she learned the contrast of being impatient and not being in tune with what her body really needed. She went against her medical team's instructions for her drainage tubes and paid a price for her impatience. She candidly shares her experience in a way that makes each of us recall when our own impatience took a toll on our well-being.

One of the most amazing gifts we have on earth is the gift of prayer. A diagnosis of breast cancer oftentimes makes us question our faith, both faith in God and faith in ourselves. We question the power of prayer, how prayer works, and we question if we really know how to pray. Perhaps this is the ultimate lesson from the breast cancer experience is what conclusion or perspective we decide to apply. I was deeply touched in Diane's chapter about prayer and how a group of amazing people applied the practice of prayer for her friend Sharon. Praying from the heart is one of the purest forms of love. When we pray, our hearts are touched and that is healing in itself. For the remaining days of our lives, no matter how many days we have left, being touched by the love of someone else is one of the greatest gifts of life. Accepting prayer can be hard to accept, because oftentimes we are more comfortable praying or doing for someone else and not accepting prayer or kindness for ourselves.

I invite you to reflect upon your lessons in life and what the breast cancer experience is teaching you as you read this book and how your burdens can become lighter as a result of applying these lessons.

Bernie Siegel M.D., author of Love, Medicine and Miracles teaches that in order to heal from our disease, we must heal our life. Remember that healing happens on many levels and the healing that our soul wants us to have can happen in the blink of an eye, and may be different from what your current belief or concept about what you think your life must look like in order to experience joy after being diagnosed with breast cancer.

There is an irony wrapped in these lessons… all of these lessons have nothing to do with money, yet provide an enriched way of life after breast cancer, and each of these lessons have no monetary price attached to them but provide priceless value to enjoy as much as we can for the rest of our life.

May your life be touched as a result of Diane's messages. My prayer for you is that you don't let the diagnosis of breast cancer stop you from seeing and embracing the many blessings already in your own life.

Be a Thriver on your terms, in your style!
Beverly Vote
Publisher, Breast Cancer Wellness Magazine

Dedication

FOR MY GRANDDAUGHTER, Elsie Eileen Jacobs, in hope that she and her generation and beyond not have to face the challenges of a breast cancer diagnosis.

Appropriately Elsie's favorite animal is the turtle. In the wisdom of the totem, the turtle teaches us about walking our path in peace whether it's inviting us to cultivate peace of mind or a peaceful relationship with our environment and then sticking to that path with determination and serenity. Those who walk with the turtle have exceptional navigation skills. They can always find their way through anything.

Book Mission

TWELVE YEARS AGO I faced the most terrifying journey of my life when I was diagnosed with breast cancer. Hearing the word cancer connected to my body refocused my mind immediately to planning my funeral. I did not hear the discussion between my family and my doctor. I just knew that I was going to die soon.

Well I didn't die. I am here more fully alive than ever thanks to that very breast cancer diagnosis and resulting journey. In 2005, I published *From There to Here; A Breast Cancer Journey*. In a effort to help me get my mind around the path that I was called upon to walk, I kept a daily journal describing what was happening and what I was experiencing and at the same time giving voice to my feelings about those very things. The interactions with my husband, family, friends, doctors and other medical staff eventually developed into many valuable life lessons. The reading and rereading of my journal helped me to see these lessons more clearly and reinforce within me the importance of what I had learned through the breast cancer experience.

Now after twelve years of survivorship, I once again reflect on those experiences and life lessons with the enhanced awareness that only time can provide. With age comes wisdom and with wisdom comes less fear to cloud my vision. Twelve more years of living life through the perspective of a new lens given by my cancer experience emphasizes the increased importance of the life lessons learned on the journey. What is the sense of living if we do not continue to learn and grow through each day given to us? With my teaching background and attitude of gratitude with its desire to help others, the logical next step is to pass on that knowledge to make the journey that much easier for those that follow.

Breast Cancer Saved My Life is my gift of love to those facing a life-threatening diagnosis and their caregivers. The emotions, thoughts, challenges, insights and the prayers are a common part of the process of learning to come to terms with a medical encounter of this magnitude. Patients, caregivers, counselors, pastors, life coaches, medical personnel, anyone hoping to understand what another goes through when facing this type of challenge will benefit from reading this book. May my life lessons enhance your life lessons and may we pass them on to future generations so that the journey is less lonely and more filled with the spirit of love.

Introduction

"AND THEN, OUT of the black beyond, like a hawk on a rat, some nameless catastrophe would swoop into your life and turn everything upside down and inside out forever." (The Smoke Jumper by Nicholas Evans, Delacorte Press)

My nameless catastrophe has a name – breast cancer. It too swooped into my life and turned everything upside down and inside out forever. The year was 2003 and the month October. I had been having yearly mammograms since the early 70's after my mother had been diagnosed with breast cancer. The procedure had always been routine. The technician compressed my breasts a little harder one year and then maybe not so much the next. I was being watchful and taking care of me by continuing to have the mammograms. This year the routine was broken. "We need to see you back again for a magnified view of your right breast as we've found two areas of calcifications," I heard the technician say over the phone. "Here we go", was my first thought. I'd been expecting this call since 1971 when my mother was diagnosed with breast cancer. I sobbed when I told my husband that I was called back for another round of mammograms. After the second procedure confirming the areas of calcifications, the consensus was for me to come back in six months to reassess those two areas. The appointment was made for April 19, 2004. I wrote the date in my calendar and put it out of my mind as best I could. Cancer was knocking on my door but for some reason I was given another six months reprieve. I was after all taking care of myself.

The months went by rather quickly. One morning in early April as I was getting dressed, I noticed in the mirror that my right nipple seemed to be about inch lower than my left and that the right breast appeared somewhat larger in size. My Mother's words of thirty years earlier came back to me, "I watched my breast grow and change shape Diane for over a year before I gave in and went to the doctor." I was frozen with the realization and terror of what my own body was now showing. Had I been wrong to wait the six months? Should I have pushed harder for more answers six months ago? Second guessing does absolutely no good. I'd made my choice then and now must follow through on the outcome. The biopsy followed the April 19 mammogram and became my undoing. Butch was told to find something interesting to do for three hours and then come back to pick me up. I would have given anything to walk out the door with him. After he left, the dam finally broke when they asked me if I was ready to begin. All of my fear, anxiety and dread could no longer be denied. The tears flowed as my apprehension took over. A patient advocate came to hold my hand and my heart and listen as I gave voice to my anxieties. She helped me to recognize my fears and call upon my intellect to bring calm and understanding. I knew that I had a mountain to climb with no chance of finding a way around it. The best route was to get started and get it over with. Two biopsies were required with a bit of a break in between. I prayed, recited Bible verses and sang my way through the tests. Butch arrived and we headed home to start the waiting for results game.

Why do they do these tests on a Friday? It only drags out the agony of the wait. By Wednesday of the following week I still had no results. Somewhere between the hospital and my doctor's office the results were lost in transmission. My daughter and I had both been on the telephone trying to trace down answers. We were becoming more and more frustrated in our search. I was stretched tighter than a telephone wire and didn't know how much longer I could hang on without answers.

By Wednesday afternoon I finally received the much dreaded and yet at the same time longed for phone call. Breast cancer was confirmed by my gynecologist. She went on to apologize for my extremely long wait for answers. "These types of results are never given over the phone, Diane. I usually have my patients come in to the office. However, knowing that your anxiety level is so high, I felt it necessary to call you with the results as soon they appeared on my desk," she reported. She also had taken the liberty to set up an appointment with the breast surgeon for that very afternoon. I truly had expected to hear that it was breast cancer and yet upon actually hearing the diagnosis said about my body, I felt as if I had been hit in the stomach with a baseball bat.

My journey through this dreadful disease took ten months – three hundred and two days to be exact. I had a bilateral mastectomy by agonizing choice on May 13, 2004. Leaving for the hospital that morning, it all seemed so ludicrous. I was in reality going in to have an amputation of sorts – having both breasts removed. The cancerous breast left me no choice. Two tumors were found too far apart to leave much of a breast. Mastectomy was the only option. The taking of the healthy breast was my idea. After my Mom's single mastectomy, she struggled the rest of her life trying to maintain a balanced appearance. For that reason and to avoid having to face another breast cancer journey later on in my life, the decision was made to take both breasts. At the same time, I had reconstruction started with tissue expanders implanted under my chest muscles. With my decision to have both breasts taken and the fact that my lymph nodes were not involved in the cancer, I was blessed to need no chemotherapy or radiation.

The reconstruction process was completed in February of 2005 with the tissue expanders being removed and the implants put into place. I opted not to have nipples created and aureoles tattooed as my future plans did not include any topless dancing. My husband was happy just to have me still with him breasts or no breasts. My story at this point has a happy ending. I am very blessed and very grateful. I also know that my final chapter is not written. Will my cancer reappear? No one has the privilege of knowing that answer this side of heaven.

As a classroom teacher for twenty-six years, I've always recognized how the experiences of today help prepare us for what we face tomorrow. As a breast cancer patient, I again became the student learning new life lessons daily as my journey progressed. Through three hundred and two days, I wrote in my journal concerning the steps being taken, the interactions with the people around me that were taking place, and my feelings regarding all of it. With my mother's diagnosis and now my own, I was afraid for my daughter's well-being. I wrote the journal for her so if and when she was faced with the journey she would have my words to help her through whether or not I was there to help. The reading and rereading of that journal helped me to see these lessons more clearly and reinforce within me the value of what I had learned through the breast cancer experience:

The timetable is not mine

The Importance of Prayer

Being open to the different forms and ways of love.

Life is a good and precious gift.

Attitude of Gratitude is most appropriate and healthy.

The importance of being a gracious receiver.

Lifesavers come into your life so listen and trust what they have to say.

Breast cancer did swoop into my life and turn it upside down and inside out. It was a long, arduous, life-changing journey. The lessons I have learned and the alterations to my body, mind and soul have been transformational. I am comfortable with my new body. I can look at my new breasts with their fading red, purple, and white scars crossing each horizontally, and see beauty and fresh new life. I'm proud of them and the courage they stand for. I see myself as a warrior and I have the battle scars to prove it. I'm different than I was in 2003-04. I'm thankful for my breast cancer journey and for those new journeys yet to come.

I've been navigating my life since breast cancer for nineteen years now. With more living comes more experience. With more experience—more understanding. With more understanding—the greater the wisdom to share with less fear. The teacher in me reemerges ready to ponder and review those life lessons expressed in *From There to Here; A Breast Cancer Journey.* (by Diane Davies, DeForest Press, 2005) I realize those lessons saved my life and brought me through my cancer journey stronger in body, mind, and spirit, more contented and with a new perspective on life. Taking another look at those same lessons in the twelve years since my diagnosis, I have been able to look more intensely at each and discern more deeply the effects they have had on my life. I've found those same lessons hold true today with increased value and significance that only come through the passage of time. The lessons have life saving messages for those diagnosed with breast cancer as well as for anyone facing a life threatening challenge of any type as well as for you the reader. Thank you so much for taking the time to read my thoughts. My hope is that in these pages you may find some lessons or messages that will help you grow in body, mind and spirit. It is my belief that we continue to learn and grow every day of our lives. When we stop growing and expanding, we soon die.

Welcome to *A Breast Cancer Journey From There to Here* a compilation of my writings on my breast cancer journey.

Diane Davies

Part 1

Diagnosis

I Thought I Knew Life

By Carolyn Salter

I thought I knew life
Touched all the facets
Shone in the sparkle
Plumbed the depths
Clambered back to sparkle

I have known life
Learnt from experience
So why now, this
This huge challenge
Life threatening?

Did I need to look again?
Perhaps
Could I make a difference?
Perhaps

I thought I knew life
But I am learning to know it
All over again.

April 19. 2004

Day 1

I HAD MY last mammogram in October of 2003. They called me back for a follow-up mammogram two days later, October 16. Some areas of calcification were seen on my right breast. They told me that they would like to do another in six months to assess where we're at with those two areas. I set up the appointment for April 19, 2004 and put it out of my mind. Here it is April 19. How time flies when you are trying to forget.! I really hadn't given the whole thing a lot of thought until just a couple of weeks ago. I noticed in the mirror that my right nipple seemed to be about an inch lower than my left and that the right breast appeared somewhat larger. Then I remembered my Mother telling me after her mastectomy in the early 70's, that she had watched her breast grow and change for over a year before she gave in and went to the doctor. I pretty much froze with the realization and terror of what I was now seeing on my own body.

> *Now my brain went into the "What If" mode. What if it was cancer? What if I needed to have a mastectomy? What if it is too late to do anything for me? What if I die? At least I hadn't waited and watched for a year. At least, I was on my way to have the necessary*

tests. How will I ever be able to handle what lies ahead? How will my family get along without me? I don't want another woman to watch my grandchildren grow up and call her Grandma. I want to be around to see those grandchildren born, to see Krisi my daughter as a mother, to enjoy with Butch, my husband, our life well into old age. This is not fair. My Dad died of cancer at age fifty. Well at least I'm fifty six. I made it a few more years than he did! How do I learn to accept and live with this? Why me? Why now? I feel like the only person in the world with this to face. Am I being selfish? I need to slow down and take this one step at a time. That is not easy for me.

This morning has found me strangely calm as if I already knew what was coming. I drove to Stillwater listening to my Rod Stewart CD. I found I was driving slower and slower as I neared the hospital. Afraid to go ahead and knowing it was too late not to. As it was, I arrived a few minutes before my scheduled appointment. The woman ahead of me was late. When she arrived, they took her first for a normal screening. The machine needed to be changed somewhat for me as they needed to do a magnification type of screening. The technician, as I learned later, had not done the type of screening I needed before on their new equipment. She naturally wanted to get the other woman out of the way before she changed things for me. That was perfectly understandable but it drug out the agony. The pictures were taken and I was told to have a seat and the Doctor would be in shortly. It was probably ten minutes or so before he came in. I have no idea what his name was even though I'm sure he told me. He put the film on the viewer and pointed out the areas of concern. I guess I pretty much removed myself once I heard 20% chance of cancer. I heard myself say that my Mother had breast cancer and that I didn't want to wait any longer. He explained a couple of options for a biopsy to be done of which I had no idea of what he was saying. I must have agreed to something, however, as he said that was fine and we'll get it setup. He then told me that on a scale of one to five, one being benign and five being malignant, that I was about a three. *I'm no math whiz but I think the odds just changed. It must have had something to do with my Mother's cancer.* He told me to contact my doctor later in the day as he would let her know within the hour what was happening. He left and the technician asked me if I was okay. I have no idea how I replied. She said that I had been a real trooper and had cooperated with her so well that she was able to get the pictures needed on the first try. She assured me that things would all work out and could she help me in any way. I didn't even know what to ask at that point. I think I was in shock or something. My world was going out of control and I couldn't do anything but go with it.

> *I was a little upset with the technician for trying to assure me that everything would be okay. If everything was okay, why was I going for a biopsy? How could everything be okay if I have breast cancer? I know she was just trying to be helpful. I need to be alone to work through things. I've always been that way. I think I need to be alone now for a while. Being angry at the technician wasn't going to help anything or change anything. So where do I put my anger? Who do I blame?*

I got dressed and headed back into the real world. On my way home, I stopped at Target to pick up my Prempro. The clinic had already called but left no message. I, of course, called Butch immediately to give him the news. He was pretty silent. "I don't know what to say, Diane." He was not surprised either. I guess it had kind of been an unspoken thing that we both knew for a while but didn't want to give voice to. That makes it too real. I called the clinic as instructed and left a message for my doctor. Her office returned my call shortly with the appointment for the biopsy set for April 22 at 10:30 a.m. I had a ton of questions between tears, none of which the nurse could answer. She told me that I had to call the hospital to pre-register and that I should be sure and ask my questions at that time. Following directions like a robot, I called the hospital. I gave them the necessary information and did quite well even if I do say so myself. I only had to look up my social security number which I know like the back of my hand. Oh well. I begin to ask my questions again and was told that she really didn't know the answers but would transfer me to the breast center where they could be of help. I declined as I was beginning to lose it emotionally. I told her that was fine I'll just be surprised on Thursday. I made a few tearful phone calls and then decided to get busy so as not to think. I used the power washer on the deck furniture and then turned it on the mold on the cement on the deck on top of the garage. Before I knew it, it was 4:00 p.m. and Butch came home. He let me cry for a bit. I can only imagine how hard it was for him. The big macho man with a heart made of marshmallow. We just sat for awhile - together. I told him that I couldn't believe how poorly I was handling this. He reassured me that I had every right to be upset and scared - after all it was my body. *It feels so strange to be talking about it, the cancer I mean, in that way. That it's my body. It seems so unreal - like a bad dream but I don't wake up.* Butch called Krisi for me and told her that I couldn't talk right then but would try and call later. The words were not coming only the tears. Maybe later I'll be able to hold it together better and give her a call. Butch forgot to pick up his prescription so he ran into Hastings to do that and bring dinner home. I finished up the deck while he was gone. I did talk to Krisi a little later through her tears and mine. We just spent a quiet evening watching TV and I crocheted. I was exhausted physically and emotionally.

> *My family knows about the upcoming biopsy. Wow! It's really happening and it's happening to me. I feel as if I'm in a nightmare and need to wake up and have it all go away. I don't think that's going to happen. I want my life back without the threat and fear of cancer.*

April 20, 2004
Day 2

I ACTUALLY SLEPT pretty well. I was exhausted. I woke up for the first time about 5:30 a.m. That's good for me even on a good day. I started the day with Butch's arms around me in bed and had a good cry. The rest of the day went by pretty well. I visited a student teacher. I work part time for the University of Wisconsin River Falls in their Teacher Education Department where I supervise student teachers in their field experience placements. I then came home and washed the big windows in the front of the house. Sunday we had had a lot of wind with a lot of dust so outside furniture/end tables etc. needed more than dusting. So I washed them all with soapy water and dried them with a soft towel. They actually look pretty good now. Butch came home early instead of going to the seaplane base for his night out with the guys, which is his usual routine. I made a quick supper then went to Bible Study. I came home feeling pretty good and went to bed. Waking up at 2:30 a.m., I couldn't get back to sleep and started thinking which is not good. Butch woke up and held me for a while while I cried. He started to make love to me by caressing my breast which only made me cry all the harder. I'm not sure if he was trying to comfort me, provide the healing touch, say good bye to my breast or help me say good bye to my breast. The answer is probably all of the above. We finally both fell back to sleep.

I have cried so many tears that I cannot believe there is any more left in me. Butch is being here for me and I appreciate that so much. I don't even know what I want him to do or say. I'm just so glad that he is here.

Diane Davies

April 21, 2004
Day 3

I HAD AN appointment with Nancy, my friend, neighbor and hair-dresser, this morning at 6:45 a.m. for a perm which I needed badly. I started this journal when I got home as a way to help me deal with whatever is ahead. I drove into Hastings for a few groceries and to get my watch band fixed. Working in the garden helped pass most of the afternoon. I moved hostas from down below to the bed to the west of the garage. That was a real workout with the shovel and wheelbarrow. The harder I work, the more I'll be able to sleep is my plan. I talked to Faye, my friend and my brother's wife, for a while this afternoon on the telephone. I then went up to the farm and worked in my garden there for a while. Bob and Bub, friends of ours, and Butch cut some brush and had hotdogs at the shop over the bonfire they created. I talked to Krisi for a while and cried again.

This waiting is getting to be way too long. I wish tomorrow was over and I knew what I was facing. I think I'll take a Tylenol PM before I go to bed tonight. I already have a headache from crying. I know where I'm at and where I want to be and the only way to get there is straight through this thing whatever it is. And that is the

24

hard part - not knowing what I am facing. The biopsy tomorrow is the next step in this journey I'm taking. I wish now that I would have asked more questions. At the time, they didn't come. I couldn't get beyond the word CANCER. As my mind settles around this, the questions materialize. I have made a resolve not to hold anything back and to ask for what I need both here at home and at the hospital. If I don't tell people what it is I need, I can't expect them to read my mind and respond to me. That will not be easy as that is not a part of who I am. I do need to practice that and I will. I keep looking at the clock and wishing it was twenty four hours later.

April 22, 2004

Day 4

THIS FEELS LIKE "Judgment Day". The sun is shining brightly and spring continues to come in spite of the turmoil inside me. I took a long shower letting the healing water calm my nerves. Butch left early to visit the gravel pit in Hastings with a promise that he would be back by 9:00 a.m. or earlier. My appointment is at 10:00 a.m. at the hospital breast care center. It's only 7:00 a.m. This will be a long morning. Checking my email I read the Daily Guidepost Devotional for the day. As in so many times in the past, the reading appeared to be there just for me:

Hebrews 12:1-2

"Therefore, since we are surrounded by so great a cloud of witnesses, let us also lay aside every weight and the sin that clings so closely, and let us run with perseverance the race that is set before us, looking to Jesus the pioneer and perfecter of our faith, who for the sake of the joy that was set before him endured the cross, disregarding its shame, and has taken his seat at the right hand of the throne of God."

Paul wrote, "Forgetting what lies behind and straining forward to what lies ahead, I press on toward the goal for the prize of the heavenly call of God in Christ Jesus."

Philippians 3:13-14

The author of the devotional, Steve Biggers (Oklahoma, U.S.A.), went on to talk about running by a lake near his home. He described one long stretch where he had to run close to the water's edge. When the cold wind blows across the lake, this part of the run becomes the hardest. Here is where he wanted to stop and lie down. But he has learned if he keeps moving he is eventually out of the way of the cold wind. He then goes on to relate this to his Christian faith by recounting times in his life, tough times, when painful experiences weakened his resolve. "But as I have become older and more mature in my faith, I have come to realize that God is always with me—during the happy times and during the sad times, during the easy run and the cold, windy stretch. There will always be times when my difficulties seem too much and God seems far away. But if I persevere, my faith grows, and I feel a renewed sense of God's presence in my life."

Coincidence? Or God at work in my life? A strange calmness came over me. Butch came home earlier than I'd expected and the time passed. We finally got in the truck and headed for the hospital. We found the breast care center and I filled out some paperwork. The receptionist answered my first question by informing me that the results would be available in forty eight hours but that since today was Thursday, I would have the results from my doctor sometime on Monday. That was not what I wanted to hear. *I felt like I had been kicked in the stomach.* They put us in a darkened room and showed us a video regarding breast cancer and the procedure I was about to have. It listed a number of high risk factors of which I swear I had all but one or two. (*That was real comforting.*) When it ended, I looked over at Butch who has this wonderful gift of relaxation. His eyes were shut and he appeared to be sleeping. I felt as Christ must have felt in the Garden. He immediately got my sharp elbow in his side and elbowed me back with a grin. "I'm awake!"

Catherine, my technician for the procedure, Mammotome I think it's called, (Why do I keep spacing this stuff?), came in for me and said they were ready. She told Butch it would be about two and half hours and told him to have a seat in the lobby. I knew that wouldn't work. He'd be off keeping himself busy to pass the time. I didn't blame him. I wished I could just leave my body there for the procedure and join him in however he was going to pass the time.

We started off with another mammogram as they wanted their own pictures not the ones from the clinic. Catherine made the mistake of asking me if I had slept last night. The cold wind started blowing and the flood came. All of the tears that I thought I had cried came back again and I dissolved into a puddle. She moved me into the "core" room where the procedure would take place and called for a patient advocate who came almost immediately to comfort me and assure me that I was reacting very normally. She told me it was okay to be scared and concerned. She related that 80% of the procedures done here come back benign and for the other 20% they have options and methods of dealing with the disease that have pretty wonderful outcomes. I really felt sorry for the two girls. They were trying so hard to comfort me. They continually rubbed my arms and shoulders in compassion. I was on the cold wind side of the lake and knew that the only way to get back into the calm was to persevere and keep moving. No stopping here. I had my moment of self pity now it was time to move on. The radiologist came in and Catherine introduced him to me. He never shook my hand or made eye contact with me which I thought was rather strange. Perhaps my red swollen eyes were too much for him to handle. He did talk somewhat to me during the procedure but it was very obvious that patient communication was the job of Catherine. Believe it or not, I was basically pretty quiet and only spoke when asked a question. That is not normal behavior for me.

Catherine asked me if I was ready to start. I had to lie on a table on my stomach with my left arm up beside my head and my right arm tucked beside my right side. My head was turned toward my left arm and my right breast hung through a round hole in the table. The table was like a hoist in the mechanics' garage that lifts the car so it can be worked on from underneath. Only I was the car and my breast was what was to be worked on from underneath. As in a mammogram, the breast is compressed in a vice like device so it and/or you do not move. Believe me, there was no way that I was about to move. The most uncomfortable part was the stiffness that began to set in after being in one position for a long period of time. Two biopsies were to be done on the two areas of my breast that were questionable. I did get to roll over and rest between procedures which helped with the stiffness. I did an awful lot of praying as I lay there listening to the soft music they had playing in the background. I said the Lord's Prayer, Psalm 23 and any other prayers and verses I knew by heart. Some of them I repeated over and over again. I felt very little during the procedure. They used lido cane to numb the breast but being under all that compression for a period of time had to help with the numbing process as well. The only sensation I had was of a little tugging and pulling accompanied by the noises of the machine at work. When they finished, I had a little difficulty trying to move. She told me to roll over and I said, "Oh yea, right! I'm trying. Give me a little time to get this body moving."

Catherine was much more relaxed now that the procedure was over as I'm sure I was. We needed to take two more mammogram pictures before I was ready to leave. In the process, my breast started to bleed again and few drops of blood landed on my light colored pants. Catherine smiled and joked and laughed with me as she bandaged and bound my breasts for support and tried to clean the blood out of my pants. She told me that my core samples were there on the counter if I wanted to take a look. Two round dishes held four samples each of my breast tissue. I remembered the old potato guns that used a small round core of real potato as ammunition. That is what

29

the samples looked like to me. They were about an inch and half long and an eighth of an inch in diameter. So there I was a sample in a dish in the hands of the lab and God.

Catherine teased Butch about taking me out for lunch and not letting me do any work or heavy lifting. He of course asked for how long and she replied that at least three weeks would work. Then laughed and told him that at least the rest of the day would be fine. She wished us good luck as did the receptionist and we walked outside into the warm sunshine of a beautiful day. The cold wind I'd been feeling was gone now for a bit but I knew it would find me again as the waiting for Monday began. This was only Thursday afternoon.

I slept most of the afternoon until Krisi came for a tearful visit. She was upset about all of the waiting that I was required to do. We talked for a long time and held hands and cried. I know it made me feel better. Jeff, my son- in-law, brought pizza for dinner and so went the evening. Tylenol PM helped me sleep through the night.

I'm glad that this day is over with and I hope never has to be repeated.

The Starting Line

By Carolyn Salter from
Hurdles are for jumping

So here we are
At the starting line
Lining up
To jump the hurdles
Not our choice
Not even our sport
In some cases
But hurdles we are jumping
So bring on the starting gun
Let's get a run at them.
Some we will not clear
But we will knock them down
And we will reach
The end
Proudly.
We will jump the hurdles
And our families
And our friends
Will cheer us on
All the way
To the finish line.

April 23, 2004
Day 5

I COULD REMOVE the ace bandage this morning and the other wrappings but I needed to leave the two strips that actually covered the incision spots for three to five days or until they fell off. The tape holding the gauze in place tore off a layer of skin as I pulled it away. That burned a bit but I survived. That in fact hurts more than the biopsy area and will take a little time to heal.

Butch was flying the Super Cub up to Tower today to deliver a part for our Cessna 185. He had asked me to go with him. We planned to leave the Cub for a few repairs and fly home the 185. It was a good trip. The Cub was tossed around a bit by the wind the farther north we traveled. Some of the bumps were pretty jarring, but I held my arms tight around my breasts to keep them from bouncing too much. Jim and Brenda, friends of ours, were on their way up to their cabin on Lake Vermilion in their airplane and radioed that they would wait for us at the Tower Airport and we'd go for lunch. It was good for both Butch and I to talk with them about what we were facing and about how hard the waiting was proving to be. We then went to the fish hatchery and the ranger showed us around and explained the walleye spawning process and how they were helping nature to be more successful. It was pretty interesting to see the huge walleye swimming in the pens. Butch never seems to catch any that size. It was also good to be busy and have something else other than myself to think about.

After we arrived home, we decided to stop in and visit with Rita and Joe, Butch's sister and her husband who live just up the hill from our house. They were about to have a bonfire and burn a little brush and a few hotdogs. It was a relaxing evening. And the waiting continues…

> *Talking with family and friends is proving to be most helpful for both of us. The more I share with others, the easier it is becoming for me to talk about the possibility of cancer. I won't be able to do this alone. I need the help of all including God.*

Saturday, April 24, 2004

Day 6

ANOTHER DAY OF waiting… Krisi has school this weekend so she won't be around to spend some time with me. She is working on her master's degree in education through St. Mary's. Butch called from the shop and had me come up to choose the lettering for our boat. Crystal, a friend and local artist, was there to start the painting and needed to know our style choice. I stopped at Rita's on the way home and we had a nice heart to heart discussion. We both cried and hugged and cried some more. Butch and I met Bub in Prescott for lunch. We shared our news. It really helps me to talk about it. I don't feel so alone. Butch needs to know that he has friends that are willing to listen as well.

Butch told me that in the night I had given him quite a start! He said that I just sat up and let out the most blood curdling scream. The subconscious mind is a real mystery. I must have been dreaming something awful. I don't remember but I do remember him holding me tight until I stopped crying and fell back to sleep. *He's taking the in sickness and in health vow very seriously. I'm so thankful for his love and care.*

Tomorrow is Grandma's eighty fourth birthday and if the weather cooperates we're planning a "burnout" with more hotdogs, beans, and such. Target was next on my list as we needed a gift for the party. And so went the afternoon.

While I was out doing errands, Karen C., another friend and member of my "Sisters In Spirit", dropped off a "Happy Thoughts" planter of pansies. I'm sorry I missed her visit. I will phone her this evening.

> *I'm finding that the busier I am the less time I have for thinking and the faster the time goes. It is comforting to have family and friends share their love with and for me.*

Sunday, April 25, 2004
Day 7

ANOTHER DAY OF waiting… I feel like the accused waiting for the jury to return with a verdict. The only difference is that I know the jury will be in on Monday.

Today is Grandma Beth's birthday and a family "burnout" is planned. Hopefully that will be enough distraction to shift my thinking to something else for a while.

> Butch, Krisi, and Jeff as well as Butch's sisters were very supportive today. Jeff hugged me and said that if it is cancer the medical community now has many treatment options with wonderful results. I guess he thinks it is cancer as well as I do. I'm beginning to realize that this whole thing is extremely hard on Krisi and Butch as well. I guess cancer happens to the whole family not just the patient. I had a few phone calls and some encouraging emails as well. It certainly helps me to have other people know what I'm facing. They can't take it away but they can give me their love and support so I don't feel so all alone. I hope I can sleep tonight. I'll take a Tylenol PM and hope for the best.

Monday, April 26, 2004

Day 8

THE DAY IS here. My heart jumps every time the phone rings and its only 7:30 in the morning. I keep wishing the day away so I would know one way or the other. If it's malignant, let's get on with it and devise a plan. If it's benign, let me get on with my life. Right now I feel so on hold from everything. Nancy called and asked me what I had heard. I know what a tough call that was for her to make and I appreciate it so much. Krisi just called to tell me she was coming to spend the day with me. She had called a sub and was on her way. She teaches seventh and eighth grade English at a middle school not too far away. What a blessing. It will be nice to have some company and a hand to hold. Butch said he would try to be home by noon. I continue to pray. I do not feel abandoned.

It's now 4:45 p.m. and I still don't have any answers. I called the breast care center this morning and talked to Shelly the receptionist. She told me to call back at 12:30 p.m. as it usually takes until noon for pathology to get their reports out. I also called my doctor's office and left a voice mail message asking her to call me as soon as she had any information. I related how difficult the waiting was again. Butch came home around noon and spent the afternoon with Krisi and I.

About 1:30 p.m. Shelly from the breast care center called back to tell me that she had talked with pathology and that the test results would not be done until 5:00 or 5:30 p.m. today. They would then be faxed to the doctors office. That probably means I will not hear until sometime tomorrow. She suggested I call the clinic again and inquire how that would be handled and when would I know. My doctor does not have office hours every day either so I called again relating the new information that I had. Again I left a voice mail. About 3:30 p.m. Krisi called the clinic and asked to talk to a real live person and again had to leave a voice mail. As of yet, I have heard nothing from the clinic. I've about given up for today. Krisi sobbed in my arms before she left. I sobbed right along with her.

> *This is so hard for me and yet I see Krisi suffering even more than I am. She keeps saying how ridicules this whole waiting game is and how rude and uncaring of the medical profession. We need to have an answer SOON and yet it will come in its own good time. Thursday feels like a lifetime ago. I wonder if I'm over reacting to this whole ordeal. What if it is not cancerous? Then again what if it is? I still do not feel abandoned. I have the love and support of my family and friends. God will give me His answer when He is ready I guess.*

Watching

By Carolyn Salter from
Hurdles are for jumping

Sometimes I think
It is harder to watch
Someone you love
Suffering
Than to be that person.
If it were me
I would know
How I felt.
I could deal with it
But I am resigned
To watching
From the sidelines
And hurting twice
Once for you
And once for me.
I wish I knew a way
Beyond that.
For it is agony
Watching you
Loving you
And unable to fix
The situation.

Tuesday, April 27, 2004

Day 9

Have you ever just known something? It feels even like more than a premonition about something - you just know. As I walked up to the farm this morning, I was remembering when I was in ninth grade. I was up for carnival queen that winter and when I came out on the stage the night of the coronation, I "knew" that I was the winner. I don't mean in a haughty, proud, arrogant way. I mean I just knew. I had that same feeling last week when we walked into the breast care center for the biopsy. I just "knew" that my mass was malignant. I remember thinking how this was just the beginning of my walking into and through this trial that I was about to face. I asked God to give me the strength to face whatever was about to come my way.

THE PSALMIST WROTE, "Turn to me and be gracious to me, for I am lonely and afflicted. Relieve the troubles of my heart, and bring me out of my distress." Psalm 25:16-17 (NRSV)

This is the Daily Guideposts' reading for today.
Even though I still have not heard my results, I've decided
that enough is enough. I'm choosing to live my life as the
true gift it is and not obsess and continue to worry over
whatever it is in my breast. I will know when I'm suppose
to know and will handle it at that time. I've wasted too
many days being overly concerned regarding this issue.
It's hurting me and my family way too much and it is
time to move on.

Last night at 5:45 p.m. Donna, my doctor's nurse, called from
the clinic. She told me that the doctor had just gotten off of the
phone with pathology and that they did not have the results. My
doctor does not work on Tuesday but the doctor on call has been
alerted and will call me as soon as the results are in. Donna was most
sympathetic about the length of my wait. She touched on my pre-
liminary reports, the mammogram, and said that things really looked
pretty good. She related to me that if she could personally run and
pick up the results she would but they were not ready and we'll just
have to wait no matter how hard it is. *Bless her heart. I felt that she*
really did care.

So here we are. It's Tuesday morning and my life
must go on. I encouraged both Butch and Krisi to go to
work. They listened to me and decided to do just that.
I have more energy than I've had for the last week. The
sun is shining and I want to get out in my gardens.
The weeds are already getting ahead of me. I know that
whatever the results bring, we will be able to handle the
days ahead. I have the love and support of family and
friends and with God beside me I will make it. Perhaps
this is my lesson - perhaps this is where I needed to arrive
on my journey through this trial.

I called the clinic this morning and left word with the nurse of the doctor on call to be on the look out for the test results. At about 1:30 p.m., I called the breast care center and was told that the results had been faxed last night but they were faxing them again at that very moment. I waited until a little before 4:00 p.m. I knew once again we were closing in on the end of the working day and I would need to wait once more over night. Krisi came about that time and called the clinic to find out when my doctor would be in again. She works on Wednesday from 8:00 a.m. until 4:00 p.m. she was told. She then called and made an appointment for me to see her the next afternoon. The appointment is set for 3:15 p.m. Krisi had to pick Jeff up at 4:30 p.m. so she was on her way. Butch had the real estate tax valuation meeting at the town hall so he left also. The phone rang about 4:45 p.m. and it was the doctor's assistant that was on call for my doctor. She asked me about the report that I was looking for - was it an old test result or what? I pretty much lost it at that point and began sobbing and hollering into the phone. I was not very professional I'm afraid. I related the entire story again and she told me that they did not have the report. I explained that the hospital had told me the results had been faxed last night and then again at 1:30 p.m. today. She said that their fax machine must not be working because they did not have the report. She promised me she'd call pathology and get to the bottom of it and then get back to me. In about a half hour, she called back to tell me they had the results and that I needed to come in to talk to my doctor tomorrow. She talked about changes in the tissue and pre-cancer cells and early stages. "So it says that it is malignant?" I asked. She replied, "No, I didn't say that." She explained that the doctor on call feels that since she does not know you at all, that it would be better if you'd come in and talk to your own doctor tomorrow. I told her that I had a 3:15 p.m. appointment already and she offered to try and find me an earlier appointment. She double booked me at 11:15 a.m. and reassured me that my doctor would discuss treatment options at that time. I thanked her and hung up.

> *It doesn't seem quite right that a person has to call and call and argue their way into finding out test results. I'm disappointed with my clinic and the hospital. I was not asking for special treatment just sensitivity to my needs.*

When Butch came home, I shared what had happened. We both cried for a bit. He told me that I needed to have a positive attitude and move forward. He's right. He made me go with him to pick up a few things and a pizza.

> *Butch is sensitive to my needs and holds me while I sleep, or try to sleep. It must be difficult to walk in his shoes as well. I appreciate his being there for me. I will try to recover my positive attitude. I'm scared to death of what lies ahead. If they wouldn't tell me over the phone, it is very obviously bad news especially since they wanted to have me talk to my own doctor. I guess my world is stopping but that doesn't mean that the rest of the world will stop as well. That's a bitter pill to swallow and not very positive.*

Getting The News

By Carolyn Salter

I watch my life
Like a slow motion movie
The actress
Mouthing fear
Disbelief
But this actress is me
Not acting.

I am separate
Yet still aware
This is me
Getting the news.
Looking aghast
Seeing the mirrored faces
Of those I love
Crumple
Surely this is not me
Invaded by cancer?
I am still as I was
As I am.

Then the two "mes" merge
Truth dawns

Life threatened
Life perhaps shorter
I might die
I must face it.
And in the knowledge
As the full force hits
I, too
Crumple

Wednesday, April 28, 2004
Day 10

I WOKE UP about 3:30 a.m. and couldn't get back to sleep. I finally got up about 4:00 a.m. and cleaned up my desk. I had a few bills to pay, flex dollars to apply for, and a ton of filing to keep me busy until Butch got up a little after 6:00 a.m. He left for Shakopee and will return to go with me to the doctor's office. We'll stop and pick up Krisi on the way. She continues to face this bravely. I know how difficult it is for her. I'm glad she has Jeff's shoulder to cry on. Our dog, Shady, and I went for a walk which is good therapy and praying time. I then came back to my journal.

The telephone rang at about 10:15 a.m. It had been ringing all morning and I had been choosing not to answer. This one I picked up for some reason and it was my doctor. For a brief second or two I thought perhaps she was calling to tell me that the test results I had been given were not mine, a last glimmer of hope for a reprieve. No such luck! She started out by apologizing for her staff and the way things had been handled regarding my test results. She assured me that her unhappiness over this had been shared with the staff and that it would not happen to another patient. "I know that doesn't help you much," she continued to say. I did relay to her my disappointment in the handling of this matter with both the clinic and the hospital. She apologized again. She expressed a desire to meet with me at 11:15 a.m. as scheduled if I so desired, but that she was prepared to talk about the test results over the phone now knowing how anxious I was becoming. She also explained that she had taken the liberty to set up an appointment for 2:15 p.m. this afternoon with a breast care specialist with the clinic. She explained that I did have breast cancer and that she'd try to answer my questions as best she could but that the specialist would be better able to lay out my options for me this afternoon.

Butch came home about 10:30 a.m. thinking we were leaving for the clinic. We had a few hours to kill so we decided to deliver my car to the tire place in Hastings. We dropped it off and drove out to Apple Valley to pick up my new wheel. I had hit a good sized pothole this spring and bent my existing wheel. Then back to Hastings to drop the new wheel at the tire place so that they could mount the new tire on it. Well now it's noon. Butch suggested the Bier Stube for a burger. I told him that I was just not ready to face people and that I'd rather go home. I could tell that he wanted me to get out and about but I was just not ready. He complied with my wishes. We came home and made a sandwich and then left for the next part of this ordeal.

The breast specialist is a short little guy with a chuckle just under the surface ready to bubble over at any time. I felt pretty comfortable with him and Joanne, his nurse, pretty much from the beginning. My doctor told me he was a straight shooter and would cut to the point. She said he's honest and good and a skilled surgeon. She advised me to ask any and all questions and that he would answer them straight on. Her assessment was correct. He did a double take when he came into the room and saw three of us sitting there. He asked if this was the whole family and chuckled about there being a dog that had to stay home. He was right. He very tenderly explained my situation to me asking me questions along the way to make certain that I was comprehending what I was being told. He answered

Butch's and Krisi's questions just as carefully. He drew diagrams to help us understand my condition and was very patient as Krisi took careful notes regarding our conversation.

He asked me many questions about my history; when did I start menstruating, how many children, what age when the child was born, when did I reach menopause, family history of breast cancer, did you take birth control, do you take HRT, etc. When I told him that I was on Prempro, he told me to stop taking it immediately as the estrogen feeds the tumors. I told him that that would be very difficult for me as I had tried to do just that less than a year ago. My hot flashes and night sweats returned with a vengeance and I slid into depression. I cannot go off of that without something else to help me through I told him. I think he could see how agitated I was becoming over that whole issue. He just very calmly told me that I would be able to address that issue at a later date and deal with it separately from the cancer. He went on to say that I had two separate areas of my right breast that both show similar cancer. They are however not close enough together to take them out with a golf ball. He then laid out the treatment options:

1. Lumpectomy– cannot do because of the two areas not being close enough together. They would have to take too much in order to be successful.

2. Mastectomy of right breast

3. Mastectomy of right breast with reconstruction

The lymph nodes on my right side will be evaluated during surgery. If they are not involved, reconstruction could take place then. If they are involved, radiation and chemo would happen first. The reconstruction would be at a later date.

Chemotherapy– at this point not projected as needing it but the lymph nodes will tell the story.

Tamoxifen (anti estrogen) would be an option to help prevent cancer from coming to the other breast.

I had many questions about that other breast. The surgeon explained that of women who have had breast cancer in one breast the likelihood of developing cancer in the other breast is 1% a year. Out of one hundred women that meet that criterion, one would develop breast cancer each year. He said when your eighty, that's not too bad. But when you're fifty six, it gives you something to be concerned about. I asked if it would be possible to have both breasts removed at the same time. We discussed the pros and cons of taking that kind of action. I explained about my mother having one breast removed and never being really happy wearing a prosthesis. It would slide around and made her feel out of balance. She had difficulty finding and wearing clothes that would hide that imbalance. The surgeon felt that I would probably experience that same sort of thing as I was not a small breasted woman. Reconstruction could be done but it would be difficult to match up with my existing breast size and shape. After we discussed the issue more, he recommended that I have both breasts removed and reconstructive surgery done at the time if no complications with the lymph nodes occur. They set up an appointment with the plastic surgeon on May 4, 2004. He suggested that I raise my questions again on Tuesday with the plastic surgeon and get his opinion as well. After that appointment, I must call Joanne, his assistant, with my decision so they can schedule surgery with the right amount of time.

I asked the doctor if he would do me a favor while I'm out for surgery. He grinned. I asked him if he would pierce my ears and put earrings in. He said, "You're kidding? You are not kidding!" He laughed and confessed that he had very little experience in piercing ears but if I'd mark where I wanted the holes, he would do it. I could tell by the look on Butch's face that we'd be discussing that one again as he is not a fan of any kind of piercing.

We left the clinic armed with books, pamphlets, and appointments. I now at least knew what I was facing and knew that I had some big decisions to make with the help of God, Butch and Krisi.

The Cancer Journey

By Carolyn Salter from
<u>Hurdles are for jumping</u>

We are on a third class train
Lurching menacingly to our destination
We know not where.
We chose neither the journey
Nor the means of travel
But we must go, nonetheless.
The journey is frightening
Many awful happenings along the way.

How will we regard the scenery?
With interest?
With horror?
With disbelief?
And what about the other travelers
And those who accompany them?

Will we help them if they have difficulties
On the train?
And what if their destination is not where
They want to go?
Can we help those left behind?
What will we learn?
Can we actually enjoy the trip?

We are on a third class train
Lurching to our destination
How we use this journey
Is up to each one of us.

When I was confirmed, our minister gave me this Bible verse; Psalm 46:1 "God is our refuge and strength, a very present help in trouble." My fifteen year old brain couldn't get around that one at the time. I was a little insulted feeling that he thought I was going to be in trouble a lot in my life. My fifty six year old brain tells me that he was a very wise man. Every life has its troubles and God is a wonderful place of refuge and strength and Who I want in my corner now and in all of life's other troubles as well.

Mastectomy— surgical removal of a breast. What an ugly word and what an ugly meaning. Cancer is another ugly word. How do I decide what to do? It all sounds so terrible. The end result of cancer untreated is eventual death. Mastectomy, surgical removal of a breast, an amputation of sorts results in more life, more time to spend with Butch and Krisi and Jeff. More time to perhaps see grandbabies come and grow. More time to enjoy what we've worked for all of our lives. Do I really have a choice? Do I have one breast removed and then live in terror of the next mammogram, the next lump, the next cancer? Do I have them both taken and live with no breasts? What does reconstruction look and feel like? Do I really need breasts at this stage of the game? Would I be happy flat chested? Would Butch be happy with a flat chested wife? I've never been happy with my large size anyway. This seems like an awful way to get that changed. Questions, decisions, decisions, questions. Life was easier before all this came up. I wonder how much time I have to make my decisions. How much time do I dare take to make my decisions before it's too late? Is it too late already?

Thursday, April 29, 2004
Day 11

THE FOLLOWING IS the email I sent out to a few of my friends. It was easier to put it together once and send it out.

"Breast cancer, mastectomy, harsh words. They are even harsher when you are talking about your own body. I'm working at getting my mind around all of this. I saw the breast care specialist yesterday afternoon and we tentatively have surgery scheduled for May 13, 2004. It will be at Lakeview Hospital in Stillwater. If the lymph nodes are not involved, I will have reconstructive surgery at the same time. We will not know that until sometime during the surgery so I won't know it at all until afterwards. I have a 99–100% chance of survival. Even so, I'm scared.

For those of you who like facts I'll share this with you from a book given to me yesterday called; Breast Cancer by Vincent Friedewald, M.D. and Aman U. Buzdar, M.D. This is what is says about the type of cancer I have:

"Ductal Carcinoma in Situ (DCIS)

DCIS is breast cancer at its earliest stage. In situ is a Latin term meaning that the tumor is confined "in place". It is located entirely within the ducts and has not penetrated the duct walls to invade the surrounding breast tissue. But DCIS is cancerous. And it may spread widely through ducts, affecting a large area of the breast.

These tumors, also known as intraductal or noninvasive ductal carcinomas, usually are first found on mammograms as microcalcifications, which are little specks or dots of calcium. (That's what I had in October.) They rarely form lumps and cannot be easily found on physical examination.

DCIS accounts for about 10% of breast cancers."

I have DCIS in two different areas of my right breast which rules out a lumpectomy because it covers too big an area. That leaves me with mastectomy. I really have no choice. If I do nothing, I will die of cancer and I'm not ready to do that just yet. I have way too much to live for and look forward to. So my enemy is DCIS and I have just begun to fight. Pray for the wisdom of the surgeons and that the lymph nodes are not involved. I'll keep you posted. Thank you all for your love and concern and prayers."

I talked to Obid, our pastor, today as I'm suppose to read the scriptures on Saturday at Carrie & Frank's wedding. Carrie is a long time friend of Krisi's. She is like my second daughter. I want to be there for the kids and do a good job. I figured the more people I could see in person before then the better I would be able to handle things. Saturday is not about me and I want to be able to support Carrie and Karen, my friend and mother of the bride, on that day. Obid said that he and Margo, his wife, would come over tonight at about 7:00 p.m. for a glass of wine and a good long talk and cry if necessary. Not to worry!

I did pretty well tonight with Margo & Obid. Butch was home also and I found it very comforting to talk about this whole ordeal with the three of them. We cried a few tears and laughed a few good laughs. We discussed my options and I felt very supported and loved. I told Obid that I would not be in church on Sunday and he assured me that he would pray for us "sinners" anyway whether or not we were there. Then he just grinned. They left with a few tears and hugs and returned fifteen minutes later for Margo's purse. I guess I'm not the only one upset by this!

Sleeping through the night is tough for me. I can fall asleep pretty easily but then I wake up at 1:30 a.m. or so and cannot get back to sleep. The night monster thoughts of the "What if… " variety keep me awake. I've started taking Tylenol P.M. so at least I make it until about 5 or 5:30 a.m. That helps tremendously.

> *It's real. I have breast cancer and I will be having a mastectomy. My emotions are on a rollercoaster ride. I feel like my life has been put in a box and someone is shaking that box as hard as they can. I continue to pray for strength to face what lies ahead of me.*

Friday, April 30
Day 12

TONIGHT IS CARRIE & Frank's rehearsal dinner. I'm reading the scriptures and my hope is that I can keep it together. I've been asking for strength all day. One of the devotionals I read today was on Psalm 91. This Psalm is the basis for the song "On Eagles Wings" which is sung at so many funerals and weddings. The song and the sight of an eagle always makes me feel secure and loved. The eagle symbolizes wisdom and strength so I suppose that is why it is our national bird. There is something about seeing an eagle in flight that is so awe inspiring and reassuring that "God is in His Heaven and all is right with the world." Living on the bank of the St. Croix River, keeping our sea plane on the Mississippi and having the privilege of owning a cabin on Rainy Lake in Ontario, we see and hear eagles daily. I've gotten so that I look for them as we taxi out on the water for takeoff as a sign that we will have a safe flight. I generally see one soaring overhead. It seems that if I don't remember to look for one, he swoops into my line of view. I feel connected to the eagle in some way because of that. So today's devotional gave me a sense of peace.

I started thinking about that connectedness and remembered watching Walt Disney's new DVD "Brother Bear" with Butch the other day. As is now the case with many DVDs, much more is included than just the movie. There are out takes, and deleted scenes, and alternative endings to the stories. The "Brother Bear" DVD has games for the youngsters (or those that still think we are young) to play. Butch & I spent an hour or so after viewing the movie doing just that. One of the games included is called "Find Your Totem". Kenai, the main character, has arrived at a very special day in his life, the day the tribe Shaman is to reveal his totem. The totems are each represented by an animal of the forest. Your totem is the predictor of the path your life will take, what kind of an adult you are destined to be. One totem is the eagle symbolizing wisdom/leadership. Another is the bear representing love. You answer a series of questions and your totem is revealed to you. I thought I'd give it a try thinking perhaps the eagle would be my given totem. I found that I was a bear/ love just like Kenai in the story. Love is a good one to have. Without love, you have nothing. Love is what is helping me deal with this waiting time before surgery. That love is coming most importantly from family and friends. I know that my eagle is still there, however, keeping a loving eye on things and he will not let me down.

Rehearsal is at 6:00 p.m. for the wedding. I need to do this for Carrie and Karen. It was my turn to practice the readings. I started out with the Matthew 5:1-12, the Beatitudes. I was doing fine until I heard my voice begin to waver. I choked back the tears and said I would try 1 Corinthians 13:1-13, the love verses. There was no way I could read any of this. So I politely said that I would read them tomorrow and sat down. Now I had Krisi and Karen in tears as well. This is exactly what I did not want to happen. The soloist reassured me that tomorrow when the adrenaline is pumping you'll be just fine. She of course had no idea of what I was facing. I just thanked her for her concern. The rehearsal continued without scriptures. Obid had everyone start over again for one last time. When it came time for the readings, he looked my way. I knew I had to do it tonight or there was no way I'd make it tomorrow. So I walked up there, took a deep breath and read both from start to finish without looking up or out at anyone. I gave a quick curtsey and sat down. Everyone applauded and off to the dinner at the Afton House we went. I can do it. I pray to God that I can do it.

Email to Gratitude Group this morning:

> "I was just thinking this morning about a conversation we had at Gratitude (Gratitude is a small group ministry group that I lead at Cottage Grove United Church of Christ. We began by focusing on the abundance in our lives rather than the lack. This allowed us to experience the sense of fulfillment which is gratitude at work. The natural outcome of gratitude is to share with others so a ministry of outreach to our community began and continues to be our mission.) the time before last about being a generous giver and a gracious receiver. Take a look at the Daily Guidepost 2004 April 12 page 110. If I remember correctly, I said that being a gracious receiver was something that I had to work on. I guess I'll be getting my opportunity to practice just that. Thank you all for the card, thoughts and prayers. I would like to try and make our May 12 Gratitude meeting. I have a feeling I will need your strength, faith and love that day. I'll bring the Kleenexes. Love to you all."

The devotional was on Hosea 14:2, "Receive us graciously…" The author, Gail, had a neighbor who had helped her through crisis after crisis. She would send over little things like ginger ale when her family had the flu. She delivered holiday gifts and treats for herself and the children. Gail never felt as if she could ever return all the favors. It so happened that Gail and her family had to move out of state and the neighbor again showed up to help clean the house and pack the car. She brought a basket lunch for the drive as well. As the two women hugged for the last time, the neighbor burst into tears. Gail realized how much she meant to her neighbor. "By allowing her to express her generous nature, I had given her the best possible gift–being a gracious receiver.," was Gail's realization.

> *It was my realization that I too would need to learn to "receive graciously" in the months ahead. I've always been on the giving end of things. My Mother, when she was still alive, would always tell me that I gave her too much or that I did too much for her. My reply was always that she should just learn to say "Thank You" and let it be. I now need to learn that same lesson and practice what I have been preaching for so long. Lord teach me to be a generous giver – and a gracious receiver. Amen*

Saturday, May 1, 2004
Day 13

CARRIE AND FRANK'S wedding day. My sister-in-law from Oshkosh, WI, Faye, is staying with her Mother who is recovering from an illness. I spent an hour or so visiting with them this morning. Krisi and the girls had hair appointments and such and then pictures at 1:00 p.m. with the ceremony at 4:00 p.m. I planned to get there about 3:30 p.m. Jeff came and dressed here and went with Butch and me. I've never sweated getting up in front of a group as much as I did this one. I wanted this day to be about Carrie and Frank and not Diane, you know the one with the cancer. I kept praying for strength to make it through and God was there for me. Not one tear was shed by this old girl and as Dee Dee, Carrie's older sister said, "Wow! You really know how to read!" I guess that comes from teaching elementary school for twenty six years. I stayed pretty up through the reception as well. One tiny melt down when I was holding Shannon's (a high school friend of Krisi's) two week old baby. Margo and Sue, friends from church, stayed pretty much by my side and I found myself actually laughing and joking about what lies ahead. Butch tells me I've come along way with this positive attitude stuff.

I hope he's right. I have a long way to go! I know where I am and where I want to be. I just have to follow the bumpy road that will take me there. With God's help and the help of family and friends, I will make it. I'm glad the wedding is over and that I was able to do the readings. Carrie is like my second daughter. She and Krisi were best friends all the way through school. I needed to be strong today for her. Mission accomplished.

Sunday, May 2, 2004

Day 14

I HAD TOLD Obid that I would not be in church today. I went up to the farm with Butch to have coffee with Grandma (Butch's mother). The poor dear is so confused. I told her about my upcoming surgery on Thursday and then her daughter Judy had surgery on Friday. She doesn't seem able to comprehend it all. Her world has become so very narrow as she ages. Everything she is revolves around her family and that appears to her to be falling apart as we all age and have health problems of our own. In her eyes, we are kids and nothing should happen to us ever.

I had intended to walk home but got busy in the garden instead. Before I knew it, it was almost noon and Krisi and Jeff came to go up to Afton Alps and help clean up after the wedding reception. Butch and I had offered our services as well. We returned by about 1:30 p.m. and I headed back to the garden to finish weeding and edging. Butch, Jeff, and Obid cut down two black walnut trees that were in the way. Obid wanted the black walnut for lumber. By about 4:00 p.m., I was pooped and so was Butch. We came home to shower and take a nap. I turned on the TV and watched a couple of movies on the satellite.

A character in the movie was in the hospital and they showed a close up of him in the bed. I looked at that bed and thought that will be me in that bed before long. My mind started playing the "what if…" stuff again and I realized that I was scared to death.

Butch woke up and said he was going to shower and I asked him to just hold me for a while while I cried. Well the dam broke let me tell you. I was a sobbing mess. I realized that I did not want to die. I felt trapped by the whole situation with no way out except right down the middle. Butch reassured me that we can fix this and that we will. We will do this together he kept telling me and with no words left to say he just held me.

I've come to hate my breasts for what they are doing to me and to us. The pain they are causing is almost unbearable. Butch is right, however. We will get through this together. I wish my breasts would just fall off and save me the agony of the surgery and recovery. Deep down I'm just a big chicken and a big baby afraid of a little pain. If I want to live, and I do, then my only choice is to face the agony and the pain. I don't know how I'll make it to the 13th.

We had many phone calls tonight. Butch very graciously answered them all and just said that I was having a difficult time at present and couldn't come to the phone.

What would I do without his love and care? What would I do without the concerned relatives and friends that keep calling, sending cards and emails of support? Love will get us through.

What Is A Life Worth?

By Carolyn Salter

What is a life worth?
A house? A car?
More adult toys?
More than this.
Education? Knowledge?
Much more than this
A family? Friends?
Oh. And more.
A life is worth love
As much love as can fit into it.
Love from all those around
And for them
Different love for each
And caring for all things
Knowing we are all
Little parts of the whole
Small sparks of the one great flame
All connected.
Complete empathy
All part of creation
And the creator
Knowing this—
This is what a life is worth
Love.

Monday, May 3, 2004

Day 15

AGAIN THERE WERE many calls, emails, and cards of encouragement and support. I don't know how people without friends get through this kind of stuff. I received a card today from Jason (my nephew) and Carie and their family. On the outside it said, "When your life is really hectic, sometimes it helps to stop and smell the roses." On the inside, "And sometimes it helps to stomp them into the ground just to blow off steam. Hang in there."

> *Wow! Is that appropriate! Next time I get really down like last night, I'll have to stomp a few roses into the ground. I love it! I'm sure in the next days I'll have opportunity to do a bit of stomping.*

This afternoon I received a phone call from Carolyn H. She is the chair of the committee I've been assigned to work with at United Theological Seminary where I've just agreed to a three year term on their board of trustees. I had sent her an email regarding my new health concern and what that might mean for me for the next few months. Rather than reply by email, she called. Carolyn is herself a breast cancer survivor. She had her surgery eight years ago this month.

She told me of a time when she was on her way shopping before her surgery when a wave of anger hit her cold. She realized that she wanted to kill the person in the car in front of her. The anger was that strong and overwhelming. She turned the car around and headed home instead of into the parking lot. Surgery for her was about three weeks away so she signed up for an intensive three week class at the seminary. She went the first day and discovered after reading the first page of an eighty page assignment several times that she could not focus. Her mind would not go around the written words on the page. She decided to drop the course and focus on survival. She told me that that is what my job is for now—survival. That is where I need to focus all of my attention and not worry about the other stuff trying to crowd its way in to my days. The letters of recommendation will get written for my students when I can focus again on their needs rather than my own. For now, I have a big enough task and that is to take care of me. Switch to survival mode and make it happen. She suggested a book entitled; Peace, Love and Healing by Bernie Siegel. It gave her what she needed at the time of her cancer journey. I'll go online and order a copy for myself. God works in mysterious ways! I needed to hear Carolyn's message today and thank her dearly for it. I don't know Carolyn very well at this point, but I do believe we shall become friends. She told me that I sounded like I could handle this and asked if she could share my cancer story with the rest of the com-mittee so they could pray for me at their next meeting. "Yes, please", was my reply. "How can I turn down the prayers of a seminary?"

> *Carolyn certainly is an "earth angel" sent by God to calm my fears. Her message that "survival" is my job and concern for the next few months seems to have set me free from the other responsibilities that I can not focus on anyway. I needed to be given that permission and she provided it for me. The rest of my life is on hold until I get through this cancer thing and that is okay! Now I just need to put that belief in to action. That is always the hard part but I'm going to try.*

Tuesday, May 4, 2004

Day 16

I HAVE MY appointment with the plastic surgeon, this morning at 11:45 a.m. I feel a bit like I'm going on a shopping trip only this time I'll be choosing my new breasts! It is amazing how busy your brain can become between 5:00 and 6:00 a.m. Between prayer and questions to ask the doctor and wondering about the surgery and thinking about the book given to me at the surgeon's office last week, Breast Cancer by Friedewald & Buzdar. *I'm not sure where one began and the other stopped. Perhaps it doesn't matter. Perhaps it is all prayer.*

I finally sat down and read the book yesterday afternoon. I'd been putting it off until after Carrie and Frank's wedding. I needed to focus on getting those scriptures read and not on me and my health issues. Now that is where my focus can be. As Carolyn told me yesterday, survival is now my job and my main focus. I need to be informed in order to ask the questions that will help me make a decision that I will need to live with the rest of my life.

> *The book was helpful. My surgeon had done an excellent job explaining things to me in understandable terms. The book pretty much backed up what he had said. Even though my cancer is in the early stages, because*

it is present in two different areas of my right breast the mastectomy is the recommended course of action. That is where I have no choice if I want to live. My left breast is not involved in the cancer but being a woman who wears a size 40 D bra it does play into my decision. How will I look, how will I buy clothing with one big boob and one considerably smaller implant or reconstruction? What are the chances of the left breast developing cancer? And if that, then do I want to go through all of this again? The thought of facing just the mastectomy surgery blows my mind let alone the surgery with reconstruction. What will the pain and recovery be like? Will I be this freak of nature when this is all said and done? Will Butch ever want to touch me again in a sexual way? If not, will that bother me? If so, will that bother me?

Everywhere I go I feel the staring eyes of family and friends. They seem to me to be looking at my breasts. I hate that! I imagine that will continue after the surgery and will be something I'm going to have to learn to live with. I've never enjoyed the stares or enjoyed putting my body on display. That is not a part of who I am.

I know that I am loved and supported by Butch and Krisi and Jeff and the rest of our family. And I know that I am loved and supported by many many friends. Cards, e-mails and phone calls remind me of that daily. Some of Krisi's friends from work are participating in the "Race for the Cure" this Sunday and asked her if they could do so in my name. They will wear my name on their T shirts and be there in my honor. (Hopefully Krisi & I can do the same for someone else in the future.) Butch tells me that people at work call him daily on my behalf. The students and staff at United Theological Seminary are raising me up in prayer as well as the members of our church, Cottage Grove United Church of Christ. Nancy, a friend in California, has her church and three others praying for me as I know many other of my friends have done the same with their churches. Even Andy, a good friend from Rainy Lake, told Butch that he is not very good at praying but that he would try his damnest. All of that is pretty much overwhelming and appreciated. How could one woman be so lucky to have that kind of support? God truly does work through community as my experience proves to me. I hope through all of this I never lose sight of that and continue to feel and appreciate its effects on me. I hope also to be able to provide that support for others.

Karen C. called this morning and left a voice mail message regarding lunch at the Levee and a massage and/or facial that she and Deedy would like to treat me to. Here is my e-mail response:

"I was on the phone earlier today Karen when you called. By the time I got done and called you back you were on your way to the sewing lady. Sorry I missed you. I very much want to have lunch with the two of you on the 12th. I don't think I could handle the Levee and I know for certain I could not handle a massage or a facial. Right now I'm pretty much angry at my body and I don't need anymore people touching me. I hope that makes some sense to you. Perhaps later I would be able to handle that. I truly appreciate the thought, tenderness and love behind the offer. But it would only be another stressor for me at this time. Sorry. About lunch—Let's save the Levee until later this summer when we can make it a celebration. For now I think I would rather have you two just here and bring a sub sandwich or something. As the 13th gets closer, I'm having a harder and harder time holding things together. I'm afraid I would be an embarrassing mess out in public at that time. I can be a mess with you at home and not feel so bad. I know you'll both understand. Thanks again for your love, thoughts and prayers. I love you both more than you know."

I talked to my dermatologist this morning. I changed my appointment with her from May 16 to May 6. I want her to check that basal cell carcinoma thing on my neck before we get into all this other stuff. I'm having a pretty hard time this morning keeping it all together. I cry at the drop of hat. Please give me strength Lord to face this day. Colleen, a nephew's wife and friend, sent me a card reminding me to take it one day at a time. I'm trying!

My appointment was at 11:45 a.m. this morning with the plastic surgeon. We had the address and Map Qwest directions. Once we found the street we couldn't find the address. After a phone call to Stillwater Clinic with more directions given, we discovered the office building was connected to Woodwinds Hospital. The address really made no sense at all. We were just a few minutes late which really didn't matter anyway. After filling out some forms, we were led to a consultation room with a TV, couch, and two chairs. Kind of like a small living room. The nurse gave me a pamphlet on breast reconstruction, fumbled around a bit, gave me a look of pity and left the room. *I really did not want to be sitting there looking at pamphlet describing something that looked and sounded so awful. Gross was the only word that came to mind. I hated everything so far. The couch was hard, the carpet ugly, the people seemed cold and uncaring. I have breast cancer. I'm the one with a huge decision to make. This is happening to my body and I HATE IT. I hate everything that has to do with breast cancer. This is not where I want to be. It seemed like we waited quite a long time—I read the entire pamphlet and passed it to Butch to read before the doctor came in. He was dressed in a slick sport coat and tie and fancy shoes. He asked me some questions - the same things I had just written down earlier on their form. His gaze was not on my face or in my eyes but on my breasts. I felt like I wasn't really even a part of the equation - just another breast to build. I want this whole thing over and done with on May 13. I want to wake up with new breasts and get on with my life. I'm not very patient about things. I usually want something like this to be done yesterday as I don't have time for some reason to mess around. I'm angry and scared. Why is this happening to me?*

My breast care specialist/surgeon had talked about a flap procedure where they take stomach area fat and muscle and build new breasts. If I did not need radiation, that surgery could be done at the same time as the mastectomy. It would mean a longer surgery, a longer recovery, but in the end a quicker result—a done deal faster.

The plastic surgeon talked a little about that procedure but said it was very involved and would mean that I would not be able to sit up from a laying down position without rolling over on my side because I would no longer have the stomach muscles to make that happen. I would need to roll to my side and use those muscles to pull myself up for the rest of my life. *It was beginning to feel like I had no options at all.* He talked about the easier route, implants and how they could start that procedure on May 13 by inserting the tissue expanders beneath my chest muscles on each side. The muscle and skin would need to expand to make a pocket for the implant. It would be the job of the tissue expanders to make that happen. The chest muscle would also protect the implant eventually and help hold it in place. This procedure would mean a number of visits to his office where they would fill the expanders with saline solution. I would come in once a week and have more solution put in, let the skin stretch and come back the next week until I was as large as I wanted to be. Then another surgery to take out the expanders and put in the actual implants filled with silicone or saline solution. Then new nipples would be constructed and finally tattooing the aureoles around the nipple.

It sounded to me like long drawn out process. Is it really worth all of that? I WANT THIS OVER WITH. The realities of all of this are finally starting to sink in. I have breast cancer and whether I like it or not, if I want to live, I have to travel this road. I'm pretty much overwhelmed by all of this and have sunk into some major feeling sorry for Diane. I want this all over but now I have no plan of action that I want to take. I want out of this nightmare. It feels so unreal - this is not happening to me. It happens to other people out there some where. Not to me!! I feel so trapped with no way out but surgery to have my breasts and my cancer removed from my body.

Despair

By Carolyn Salter

It's a long way down to despair
And I'm getting there
Too easy to fall
When the best way is up
They keep saying that.
But the ladder is high
And I've lost my footing.
Can't climb.
I need a rope from above
Pull me up, pull me up.
I fear I won't get there alone.

It's a long way down to despair
And I'm there.
Stuck there.
But I still see a fading light
Small chink of light
Up above.
Get a toehold, a handhold
Any hold. Hold on.
Hold on.
Keep my eyes on the light
It's not easy. It's hard work.

Keep focused.
Keep climbing.
Step by step.

Who needs a ladder
With my eyes on the light?
I can make it.
I will make it!
I've made it!
I've made it!

But it's a long way down to despair,
I know
I've been there.

We left the plastic surgeon's office with no decision made. I'm not sure that I ever want to go back. When the plastic surgeon left the consultation room we were in, he told me that he would save the time for me on the 13th until later in the week. I should call his office with my decision by Thursday for sure because if I didn't want the time someone else would. When he left, I said to Butch, "Well he sure is a jackass!" Butch looked at me and said, "Oh really!?!" I got the feeling that perhaps he thought I was the jackass. *Everything feels so up in the air. I feel so helpless and hopeless about the whole thing. No plan, no direction. I just know that on May 13th I'm having my breasts removed.* I pretty much stomped out of the office behaving like a spoiled brat. Butch didn't say much all the way home. We stopped at Target to get my blood pressure medication. I cried from Woodbury to Cottage Grove to home. Butch just looked at me and said, "I don't know what to tell you, Diane. These are decisions you have to make for yourself." I asked him if he would have a problem if I decided to do no reconstruction. "Would you be upset being married to a freak of nature?" I asked. His reply, "Well Diane, I guess I don't look at it that way. I'd rather have you any way than not have you at all." That really brought on the tears.

What Is A Breast?

By Carolyn Salter

What is a breast?
Small weight of flesh
A bump or larger
Yet these small bumps
Grew
Changing me
From child to woman.
They have been touched
In love and awe

They have grown fuller
Produced milk
To sustain new life
That dependent life
Touched in love and awe.

They have been a symbol of what I am
Who I am -
Woman
Wife
Mother.

Now I am to lose one
Maybe two breasts
A no breasted woman.

Is it possible to be the same
Without the symbol?
What is a breast?
Merely the symbol
Of who I am.
But not the real woman.
She lives within.
Not relying on a breast
Or even two
To define her.

Krisi and Jeff came for dinner. Krisi asked me to ride with her to take some donations to the Stone Soup Thrift Store in Cottage Grove. We talked about my narrowing options on the drive. She was most loving and supportive as she helped me think through things. She was able to point out to me a few things that I hadn't considered before. She also helped me with decisions that were sort of already made but that I needed to justify again to myself. For one thing, I had to determine whether or not to have the left cancer free breast taken as well as the right cancerous one. I knew that I did not want to have one breast like my Mom had to deal with the rest of her life. She had difficulty dressing and always felt out of balance with one side bigger and fuller than the other side with the prosthesis. Clothes never seemed to fit right for her. She did not have the option of reconstruction in the early 70s. I shared with Krisi how I felt that everyone I talked with now was looking at my breasts and not at my face. She is so wise. She said that that will probably only get worse until this whole thing is over and behind us. "You know, Mom, you are so good about coming up with some smart aleck remarks about things, I think that's how you need to handle that feeling as well. You'll think of something to say that will get people laughing and beyond the staring," she told me. "Use your humor to make it work for you." Thinking through all of this with Krisi's encouragement, strength and love helped me tremendously. We had dinner and the kids went canoeing for a while. Butch and I walked down by the river to wait for them to return. They went into the old bar building where they have some stuff stored. Krisi loaded a few things into her truck and they left for home.

In spite of my family and their love and encouragement, I alone need to decide how to proceed with the rest of my life beyond breast cancer. How do I want to look dressed and undressed? What can I handle and what can't I handle? After asking God for His help with my decision, I took a couple Tylenol PM and went to bed. Thank God for Tylenol PM!

My family has been so desperately trying to help me and yet they realize at the same time that I must make the decisions. If I were in their shoes, I think Carolyn's poem describes how I would feel.

I Would Give

By Carolyn Salter from
<u>Hurdles are for jumping</u>

I would give
My antique cupboard
With the marks
Of many generations.
The first magnolia
In a wintry garden;
The gurgle of
A special child's laughter;
I would give
My music;
Balmy nights
Under a star filled sky;
Love collected, cherished
Over a lifetime
All this
I would give
And more
If it would take
The cancer
From you.

Wednesday, May 5, 2004
Day 17

I SLEPT SURPRISINGLY well. It must have been the Tylenol PM! I called my surgeon's nurse, with a list of questions and a few confessions regarding my poor behavior yesterday at the plastic surgeon's office. She assured me that I was normal in my roller coaster ride of emotions and that health care professionals work every day with a large range of human responses and reactions. We again discussed the fact that if I needed to have radiation the reconstruction would need to wait until later. I tentatively told her that I would have both breasts taken and reconstruction started on the day of surgery if possible. *(Wow! That's not easy to say. God help me through this! My hands are shaking along with my whole body.)* She told me to wait to call the plastic surgeon's office until she had a chance to talk again with the surgeon. Unlike others, she also told me that she would not be calling me back until after 2:00 p.m. or later that day and that I shouldn't wait by the phone for her call until after that time. That helped as I have a lot of errands to run.

Alice, a neighbor and friend, called a little later in the morning. We talked for a very long time. God answers prayers in many ways and Alice was his answer to my prayer for help. Two years ago Alice had breast cancer and opted to have both breasts removed and started reconstruction immediately. Her cancer was the lobular type somewhat different than mine but her surgery and procedure following was pretty much identical to what I was considering having done. She answered all of my questions very honestly and frankly. She told me I'd wake up from surgery feeling like I'd been run over by a truck. She had many lymph nodes taken so her arms were involved as well. She also told me that the waiting now before surgery is the hardest part. After the surgery is over and you know the cancer is gone you are better able to deal with things. Before surgery, its the fear of the unknown. After surgery, you know what you are facing and can move forward. She said she never regretted a day having both breasts taken as the worry of reappearing breast cancer was gone. She also never regretted a day of having implants. When she undresses it feels good to her to still have something there. It is not such a constant reminder as a flat chest would be. The scars are fading and actually look pretty good. She even shared with me that she very rarely wears a bra unless they are going out in public and if she's wearing something shear. She has nipples reconstructed but as of yet does not have the areole tattooing. She said she thinks she will do that yet, too. I asked her about the second surgery to remove the spacers and put in the actual implants. She told me that was just an hour and half surgery with no hospital stay. Pain pills for a day and then Tylenol or Advil. Her nipples were also formed at that time. After the initial surgery, she told me I would need help at home. She pretty much sat in the lazy boy with her arms propped up on pillows for a few days. *Alice played a huge part in my acceptance of this all. I'm so grateful for her phone call and her willingness to share such personal details. I know I have a lot to face but after having talked to Alice, I think I can do it, too.*

The surgeon's nurse called later in the afternoon to tell me that the surgeon believed I had less than a 5% chance of needing radiation. If I wanted to start reconstruction on the 13th, to go ahead and schedule it. The lymph nodes will tell the final story. I told her to go ahead and schedule for a bilateral mastectomy (both breasts) with a sentinel node biopsy and reconstruction started with tissue expanders if possible. *I don't ever want to have to face this again.*

> *I'm still terrified but at least the decision is made and the wheels are in motion. I made the call to the plastic surgeon's office. Apologized and moved forward. Now I need to work on that inner strength and positive attitude to get me through whatever lies ahead. I still dread the hours of this time before surgery. I especially dread Thursday morning and arriving at the hospital– kind of like a lamb to slaughter. However, I must remember that if I do not do this I will die. Once again I know where I'm at and where I want to be and the road I must travel in order to get there. I have a tremendous mountain to climb before I get home free - cancer free that is! I have the love of Butch and Krisi and Jeff and so many other family and friends to help sustain me. I must learn now how to be a gracious receiver of that love, support, and strength. That is a life lesson that will also be difficult for me. I pray daily asking God to continue to walk with me and stay by my side. I know He will not fail me. I know churches in our area as well as California, Australia are praying for me as well as the whole community of United Theological Seminary in New Brighton. With all that help how can I fail? Even if I need radiation and chemo I should be able to handle it with that kind of support. I know Butch was relieved with my new positively growing attitude. I still have a long way to go.*

My Sisters in Spirit (a group of women I worked with and share a close relationship) started arriving about 5:00 p.m. Vicki and Nancy came first, and then Freddie called from Ely. The two Karens arrived shortly thereafter and Nadine called. Lynn is still in Arizona but has been sending her love and support via email. We cried, hugged, talked, laughed, ate, and drank wine until about 10:00 p.m. I knew they all had to work in the morning and most had a long drive ahead to get home. I also knew they were trying to stay until Butch came home. I assured them I was okay to leave alone and that Butch would be along shortly. He was probably waiting for them to leave before he came home to give us some privacy. He was out with his own support system—Bob and Bub. The "sisters" left me with a beautiful box of healing items including Lady Godiva Chocolates, body lotion, wine and a special wine goblet just for me, Dan Moen's CD "God Will Make A Way" and two special books. Quite a comfort theme of all the things I enjoy. The box itself was a beautiful gift. They know me well.

> *It really was a most helpful evening for me. I feel very loved and supported. I just continue to wish that May 13th was behind me. This is how a condemned person must feel while waiting for execution. Alice was right. The waiting is awful!*

Thursday, May 6, 2004
Day 18

I'M FEELING PRETTY confident about my decision so far. I'm still scared but at least I'm down to one week and waiting. My plastic surgeon's assistant, Barbara, called this morning to find out if I wanted to meet with the doctor again before surgery. She was most helpful in calming my fears and dispersing my doubts. She assured me that I would be most happy with the results and that he did wonderful work. She answered my many questions and created in me a very different feeling about the plastic surgery ordeal than I was feeling on Tuesday. I told her that I didn't think I needed to see the doctor again before surgery. She told me if I changed my mind I should not hesitate to call. He's only in on Tuesday at their clinic. I'm so glad she called. She had details that Joan, his nurse, couldn't help me with.

Later in the morning Diane, a friend from Prescott, WI, called. Diane had the same surgery, removal of both breasts, in April of this year. *It's amazing how all of these people seem to be making their way into my life to lend their help and support. God at work in my life!* Diane shared her experience with me as well. She did not start reconstruction as she wanted to work this summer. She's scheduled to begin the process November 22, 2004. It was interesting to compare her more recent experiences with what Alice had to say. They were surprisingly similar.

When Carolyn from UTS called earlier in the week, she told me that my job for the next months was survival and that that is where I need to focus all of my energy and attention. Alice and Diane agreed with her. Diane shared with me how ugly her chest was now about one month after surgery and that she was looking forward to reconstruction so she wouldn't have to look at it any more. She explained about the indentations from where her breasts had been but that she was glad they were both gone and she didn't have to deal with or worry about the returning cancer - at least not in her breasts. *I feel a real bond with these women.* Carole Helgerson has also called several times. As of yet, I have not talked with her but Butch has. She is Butch's first cousin and a close friend of his in high school. She was most helpful to him and for that I am grateful. I will need to call her before the thirteenth. *My poor Mom never had this kind of support as far as I know. Her cancer occurred in the early 70's and was a pretty hush hush thing at that time. It is important to talk and keep talking and face the realities of what's ahead. I'm so grateful that I have those who have gone on this journey before so willing to share and help me along the way. My plastic surgeon's nurse said that I would be doing the same for other woman in the near future. I hope she's right.*

Butch and I flew up to Brainerd to Bill and Phyllis's cabin on Gull Lake for the weekend. The Seaplane Convention was at Cragon's just across the lake from their place. Jim and Brenda were guests of the Bryan's as well. Wip and Linda, and Ed and Marilyn from Missouri joined us for cocktails and dinner. Brenda told me that Wip had talked about having a going away party for my breasts. I reacted rather quickly and strongly that I wouldn't be able to handle that. Brenda assured me that she and Linda vetoed the idea and told Bob to back off. *I'm glad they did. Maybe later on I'll be able to handle that but right now I'm a little raw. I'm glad we came. It's good for me to be busy and have my mind occupied with other thoughts. My upcoming ordeal sneaks in to my mind often enough. It's always just below the sur-face. Hard to forget about it when its always there on your mind ready to take over your every thought. Next week is coming. Thanks be to God.*

May 7, 8 & 9, 2004

Day 19, 20, 21

PHYLLIS AND BILL'S newly remodeled cabin on Gull Lake is just beautiful. Jim and Brenda and Butch and I flew up in our separate airplanes. Bill & Phyllis had their Cessna 206 there as well. It was the annual seaplane convention at Cragans. It was a good way to pass the weekend. For the most part I think I did pretty well. Friday night I had a hard time sleeping so I opted to stay at the cabin on Saturday while the girls continued the second phase of shopping. It gave me time to sleep a little and think a lot. I did a lot of writing in my journal. What a perfect spot for that. I had nothing else that could distract me and I'm used to down time alone. I joined the group again about 3:30 p.m. for a glorious boat ride. Just like a scene out of the movie "Always" we were chased in the boat by a water bomber heading to Cragans for a demonstration. He dropped his load of water pretty much in front of our boat. We could almost touch the airplane as he flew overhead. What could be better? We had boats, airplanes, sunshine and caring friends! I had a bit of a melt down when Neil and Eileen came to say good bye and wish me well with my surgery at the happy hour before the banquet. *Talk about a way to clear the bar in a real hurry! Just start crying and they scatter. I didn't mean for that to happen but what can I say? Tears and fears lie just below the surface. I'm surprised that it hadn't happened earlier!*

We flew home on Sunday afternoon which was Mother's Day. Krisi and Jeff and Jeff's parents, Becky and Lowell, came down for a bonfire and a cookout. Krisi and Becky brought all of the fixings for the picnic including home made pie. Krisi and Jeff gave me a beautiful gold necklace. The pendant is in the shape of the breast cancer ribbon with three diamonds. The card was beautiful as well as the gift and Krisi and I both cried. *I'm so glad that her friends at school are supporting her well. She had on a pink beaded breast cancer ribbon bracelet that she had been given by her aide. It sounds like her teaching partners pretty much check in regularly and give her love and support by asking about me and my progress. She has been so strong and helpful to me that I'm glad she can be renewed by others that care about her as well.*

The guys started the brush pile on fire and had it burning hotly when a storm came up. We had 1 1/4 inch of rain and had to move the picnic in doors. The guys were soaked as they needed to stay out there until the fire was under control. The wind was doing some pretty squirrelly things before the downpour came. The storm certainly took my mind off of me for a while and that was good. Becky and Lowell must bring the rain with them from Michigan. The last time we had a huge downpour was when Krisi and Jeff were married. That day we saw 4 1/2 inches as we tried to have an outdoor reception at the farm. The reception moved indoors and a great time was had by all in spite of the rain. Today we cooked the brats on the Jenn Air inside instead of over the open fire. It all tasted wonderful since I didn't have to make any of it or do any of the work.

> *I hated to see the day end. I was beginning to get pretty nervous and uptight. Sunday night means the new week is just around the corner and what a week it would be. I'd been waiting for the 13th to arrive but now it terrified me. If I want to get on with life and over with*

cancer, I have to face whatever this week brings. The only way through this is to go straight through with head held high and eyes on the prize at the end. LIFE!

Monday, May 10, 2004

Day 22

I HAD A hard time sleeping after about 1:30 a.m. I'm developing kind of a nervous stomach as well. I guess that can be expected. I got up and read from <u>Beyond Breast Cancer</u> by for a while. It contains stories of hope and survival. I find myself in many of the stories. It's helpful to know that I'm not the only one experiencing things in this way or that. I did fall back to sleep until about 8:00 a.m. Carole, a good friend of mine, came to visit this morning with a bag full of goodies; caramel rolls, bean soup, homemade candy and rhubarb dessert. She went with me to Ptacek's to pick up a few groceries. It was good to talk to her. She is very supportive and loving.

This afternoon Butch and I drove into Hastings. I needed to get a cookbook in the mail for Marilyn Schmidt (from the seaplane convention) in Missouri and ship Amy and Erics afghan off to California. I wanted that done before I went into the hospital so that neither would get forgotten. Then I mowed the grass around the house, transplanted some hosta, planted zinnias and sweet peas by the kitchen door, and pulled a few weeds. Gardening is good therapy for the mind and soul. Also it's a good workout and should help me sleep.

The work of the summer season is beginning to play on me and I have to realize that I just can not do it all. This summer is going to have to be and look a little different around here. The weeds will wait. I'm also fretting a bit about Memorial Weekend. I do so want to go to the lake with the group as planned. That too may not happen depending on my recovery. I wonder how I will get my mind around making the list of the needed items to open the cabin for the summer. I just ran out of catsup of all things here at home. How will I ever get my mind around all the stuff needed for the lake? With no grocery store close by to the cabin, I guess we'll get along with the stuff we remember to bring. I'm going to have to learn to let go of stuff like that and not worry about it. Seems like an impossible task to me at the moment. Why do I feel so responsible for all of that? I know I'll have the help needed. No one expects me to have everything ready except me! I've always handled it and will again in time. It's so hard to learn to be a gracious receiver when you've always been the willing giver. I'm working on it.

Tuesday, May 11, 2004
Day 23

ALICE CALLED AGAIN today. What a dear. She had a couple of things to tell me. She asked me if the doctor had talked about saving my nipples to reuse. She had never heard of that before until a nurse friend of hers mentioned it. Of course it was too late for Alice but she just wanted me to know in case I wanted to ask about it before surgery. She also explained to me how they will wrap my chest after surgery using a very wide and long ace bandage and how good that feels. *I guess she doesn't want me to have any surprises. She certainly has been a big help to me with the decision making process. I hope someday that I'll be able to do the same for someone else.*

I received a note of encouragement today from Pat and Charlie, long time friends of ours. Charlie just recently had his own run in with cancer. He's finished with treatment and back to work and I guess doing very well. "Hearing the word CANCER changes your whole life—you just look at things differently. The things that used to upset us are now just minor little things," the note read. *I'm beginning to understand that already. It is so very easy for me to let the dust build or the weeds grow and go for a walk instead. I hope I can learn to*

let go of some of my anxiety about that kind of stuff through this whole ordeal. On the back of the card Pat wrote this:
What cancer cannot do…

Cancer is so limited…
It cannot cripple love.
It cannot shatter hope.
It cannot corrode faith.
It cannot eat away peace.
It cannot destroy confidence.
It cannot kill friendship.
It cannot shut out memories.
It cannot silence courage.
It cannot reduce eternal life.
It cannot quench the Spirit.

Kate, the surgery coordinator, called at about 1:00 p.m. today. I was just about ready to call the number listed on the "Preparing For Your Surgery" pamphlet when she called. My surgery is scheduled for 12:00 Noon on Thursday, May 13, 2004. I'm to arrive at the hospital at 10:30 a.m. She told me to take my blood pressure pill and the Prempro in the morning with just a little swallow of water. No food/water after midnight. Wear clothing that buttons or zips down the front and is comfortable. *Dah! The pajamas I bought, both pairs, are pullover! What was I thinking?* She asked me a bunch of questions and took down a lot of information so I guess we're all set.

I had a pre-op physical with my regular doctor today at 3:15 p.m. On the way, we stopped at Herbergers to buy some pajamas that open in the front. I now have enough new pajamas to last me the rest of my life! The physical took about an hour and a half. I had to have blood drawn and an EKG and answer a bunch of questions AGAIN! My blood pressure was a little high and my temperature was 99.1. I told them that I have been a little upset lately. This doctor also wants me to go off of the Prempro as did the surgeon. I told him that I would need something to help me with the hot flashes and mood

94

swings. We decided to give Paxil a try as well as Vitamin E. He told me to wait and start that when I get home from the hospital. So that's the plan.

Vernelle, Butch's sister, called and asked if she could be at the hospital on Thursday. Butch was a little upset with that. We talked about letting people help in whatever way worked for them and us. We both cried for a while and continued to talk. I asked him not to get too crabby with people and allow them to help. *He really seems to be having a hard time with this all tonight for some reason. I guess maybe it's getting too close. Like I said before, it's too bad it wasn't yesterday and we're on to the healing.*

Butch is really concerned about my comfort and level of pain. He plans to move the lazy boy from downstairs up into the living room in front of the new window overlooking the driveway for me. I agreed that that would work and that I wanted to be on that floor but that I wouldn't have a TV then. We decided to buy a new one and then take it to the lake later on this summer when I don't need it at home anymore. *It's good to talk and to cry and I seem to be doing a lot of both. I feel bad for Butch and Krisi having to wait through surgery. I'll not know what's happening so perhaps they will have the tougher job than me.*

> *One more day! It's getting tough and I'm getting pretty nervous. I wish they could knock me out at home and deliver me to the hospital on Thursday morning. I have plans for most of the day tomorrow and Krisi and Jeff are coming for dinner tomorrow night. That will all help pass the day. I continue to get emails, cards, and phone calls of love and support. I do feel loved. I wish it was next week at this time! It will be in seven days—right? It's hard to not be wishing my life away.*

I Am Not Alone

By Carolyn Salter

I watch the sun
Slanting rays
Fingers of light
Through the clouds
As if the fingers of God
Are touching me
Caressing me
With the knowledge
That I am not alone
All will be well
Whatever the outcome.
All I need
Is to remember
I am not alone.

Wednesday, May 12, 2004
Day 24

I WOKE UP at about 3:00 a.m. this morning and slept a little on and off since then. *I'm feeling pretty anxious today. Last night and this morning people have been calling and wishing me well. I'm finding it hard to carry on a conversation. My mind is not with them and my ears are not listening to what they have to say. I guess you could say that my focus is elsewhere—where I don't know but it's not on chit chat. Everyone is so concerned and means well. I do appreciate all of the good wishes. I just find it hard to listen to them.*

I have a busy day planned to help ease the tension. Gratitude Group will be here at 10:00 a.m. Gratitude Group is a small group ministry that I lead at our church. We meet twice a month to focus on and learn about what an attitude of gratitude can do for us in our lives. We study materials together as well as the Bible, pray and support each other in our needs. Deedy and Karen are coming at noon thirty and bringing lunch. Krisi and Piper (their puppy) will be here after school and Jeff will join us for dinner. So will go the day. I still wish it was next week at this time. *My head talk is pretty much a constant prayer for strength and courage. I really couldn't ask for more love and support.*

Prayer

By Carolyn Salter

Imagine prayers
Like little wisps
Of ethereal thread
Spiraling upward
Some catapulted by
Compulsive senders
Demanding, urging, arguing
Others pleading
Entreating
Others gentle
Beseeching
And others
Full of thanks.
Prayer threads
Coloured, glistening
Iridescent
Linking
Human to the Divine.

With all the prayers for me
I could weave a cover
Beautiful rug
To cover me,

Keep me warm
In the dark, cold times
When I am alone.

Yet not alone
For the beautiful threads
Of my friends' prayers
Shine for me
Warm me
Always.

Part 11

Surgeries and Healing

The Operation

By Carolyn Salter

I smile calmly
Ignoring the rising terror
Inside
The surgeon's knife will be poised soon
Ready to remove
Parts of my femininity
My body
Never the same again.

A little fearful now
How will I react
Afterwards?
More importantly
How will others react?

Yet part of me is serene
What will be, will be.
I will take that
And work with it.
Changing negatives to positives
Helping others
On this same road.
Perhaps even inspiring
Hopefully inspiring

Yes, serene, calm
Yet, deep inside
Just now
For a small while
A little flutter of fear
For the unknown
Yet to be.

Thursday, May 13, 2004
Day 25

THANKS TO TYLENOL P.M. I did get some sleep last night. I actually woke up pretty calm I thought. This is finally the day that I do so badly want behind me. Alice told me she remembers driving to the hospital with her family and saying, "This is so ludicrous. Here I am letting you take me to the hospital so that they can cut my chest up." I now know the feeling. It would have been better if Butch could have knocked me out before leaving the house. I'm sure that it was not easy for Krisi and Butch as well. We left the house and drove to Krisi's. She would spend the day waiting with her Dad. Jeff would come after work.

I survived the checking in process. It was most difficult to say that I'm here for a bilateral mastectomy. My name was called. Krisi didn't hear the nurse say that only one family member could accompany me right now but as soon as they had me ready they would call for the other family member to come as well. She panicked and came to the door with tears in her eyes and told the nurse that she needed to give me a hug and wish me good luck before they could take me in. The nurse reassured her that she would call her to come and join us in just a few minutes and that she would have plenty of time for hugs before the surgery.

As I started the process of getting ready for surgery, I became terrified of what was to come. The sentinel lymph node biopsy had me just as terrified as the surgery itself. Will it be negative as the surgeon predicted or would it be positive meaning I would need radiation and chemotherapy and wouldn't be able to start reconstruction until a later date? So much was at stake. Many people came in to help me get ready. I had to meet the anesthesiologist and his assistant and answer a number of questions for them. The nurse used a magic marker to put an X over my right breast. I told her that I was having both breasts taken. She excused herself and went to check on why my chart said one thing and I said another. When she came back in, she apologized and said she had misread the paperwork. *Wouldn't that be great to wake up and realize they only did half of the surgery?* I had to sign a number of forms, the IV was started, and I was given a plastic blanket that had warm air blowing through it to keep me warm. I was shivering but I don't know if I was cold or scared. Probably both. The blanket did provide me some comfort however. My surgeon came in all dressed and ready to go. He asked me if they had given me anything to calm me down. He told me that I looked like a wire stretched so far that it was about ready to pop. I agreed that that was how I felt. They had told me earlier that I would walk into the operating room and would get up on the table with help. Then they would start putting me under. My surgeon said that they were going to change that procedure today for me. He felt that I needed something immediately to calm me down. "We'll get you in there and on the table without your help," he said. My plastic surgeon was a little late in arriving and the surgeon would not start his part until he arrived. The surgeon would take about two hours to remove my breasts and the plastic surgeon would take another two hours to start reconstruction by putting in the tissue expanders and closing up. My surgeon told the anesthesiologist to start by giving me a shot of something through the IV of course. I remember saying, "It's not working. I'm not going to sleep. It's not working." (My family told me later that just after I said, "It's not working" I asked them if they could see all of the beautiful flowers. Krisi asked me what kind of flowers I was seeing and I told her, "Why, pink azaleas. Can't you see them? They're all over the place!") Shortly after that I was wheeled into the operating room. I remember being moved on to the table but I certainly don't remember much after that.

The next thing I knew I was in recovery with lots of tubes and monitors and lots of people asking me lots of questions. All I wanted to do was sleep and be left alone. Before too long I was being moved from recovery to my room in the "Women's Care Center" of the hospital. My family was there waiting for me. I remember hearing a lot of voices and trying to wake up but I kept falling back to sleep. The news was good. The lymph nodes were clear which meant no radiation and the reconstruction process had been started. Obid and Margo, our Pastor and his wife, were there as I remember hearing their voices and having someone wiggle my big toe. Krisi kissed me goodbye and went home with Jeff. I didn't realize what time it even was. All I wanted to do was sleep.

I do remember having to go to the bathroom. Two nurses came in to help me up and into the bathroom. It hurt like hell to get out of that bed and stand up. One nurse asked me if I thought I could make it to the bathroom. I replied, "I think I can." I remember her very gruffly saying that that was not good enough. Either I could do it or not. They had to know. I answered back, "All right then I can do it." I had no idea if I could or if I'd fall flat on my face. With a nurse hanging on to each side of me, we did make it across my room and into the bathroom. It was probably about five feet but felt like five miles to me. I couldn't use my arms much to help but the nurse was there and did for me all that I could not do for myself. They must have been playing "good nurse/gruff nurse" and thankfully it was the good nurse in the bathroom with me. I know that bed felt awfully good to climb back into. Butch tried to reach over the bed rails to give me a kiss before he went home. He couldn't get down far enough and I couldn't rise up to meet him. I told him I'd take a rain check until tomorrow. He just smiled and squeezed my hand and left for the evening.

Two of Butch's sisters, Rita and Vernelle, spent the day at the hospital with Butch and Krisi. I never saw them but it was a comfort to know that they were there pulling for me and helping Butch and Krisi pass the awful waiting time while I was in surgery. They did not come up to my room that I know of.

It seemed like a very busy night with someone in my room checking this and that most all night long. I drank a lot of water which meant I had to use the bathroom as well. That was not a trip I enjoyed very much.

> *I certainly felt that I was in good hands. The doctors and nurses were most helpful and caring. Thank you Lord for bringing me to this place of healing. Thank you for the staff of this hospital and thank you for the advances in medical science that have played a role in removing my cancer and giving me another chance at life.*

I Had A Dream My Life Would Be

By Carolyn Salter from
Hurdles are for jumping

I had a dream my life would be
So far from this reality
Nowhere near this absurdity
Of tubes and pieces stuck in me.

Now the simple little things
Watching how a bird can sing
Feeling sun upon my back
Knowing there's grey
Not just white or black
Believing there must be a reason
Knowing we each have our season
Feeling mine may run its course
Knowing there is always worse
Loving more than words can say
Using each hour every day
Finding more, always learning
Living life, yet still yearning
For the long life I may miss
Yet grateful for it all, and this:

Diane Davies

Cancer taught me such a lot
Cancer helped me find the plot.

But I had dreamed my life would be
Far from this reality.

Drips And Tubes

By Carolyn Salter

Drips and tubes, tubes and drips
Taking little water sips
Lying here, told to rest
Lying here with no breasts.

Drips and tubes, tubes and drips
Lots of questions on my lips
Why me, why us, why this right now
Am I supposed to know somehow
What I should do, how to react?
And where's your plan?
What's the attack?
I'll do it when the pain subsides
I'll do whatever You decide.

Ah! Drips and tubes, tubes and drips
So many questions on my lips

Jumbled Thoughts

By Carolyn Salter

Lying here
Unmoving
Sore from surgery
Can't soar just now
Grounded
Thoughts jumbled
No sense
Scents of hospital
All around
Confining
Constraining
Feeling like I've been kneaded
Into shape
Out of shape
Needed
Yes, I'm needed
By all those I love
Send my thoughts there
To be un-jumbled
So they can come back
Floating
Soaring
Settling back to me
Clear thoughts

Friday, May 14, 2004
Day 26

ALICE WAS RIGHT; I do feel like I've been run over by a truck. But the good news is that the lymph nodes were not involved with the cancer. The tumors were "insito" meaning they had not moved out of the ducts in my breast. I could stand the pain knowing that the cancer was gone from my body and that reconstruction had started as planned. I was a most happy camper.

The day passed rather quickly with doctors and nurses in and out and family and friends stopping by for short visits as to not tire me out. I even had phone calls from friends vacationing in Alaska and Wyoming. Flowers and gifts were delivered and love shared. I have never felt so loved and supported before by so many people in my life. Obid stopped by again, and we said prayers of thanks and healing. My journal writing today was hardly readable. I tried. I had four drain tubes, two under each arm, to help drain away the fluid that collects as a part of the healing process. They made it pretty difficult to use my arms for anything but just hanging there. Writing and wiping were most difficult.

By evening, I was beginning to feel pretty anxious. I was moving around better and adjusting to the drain tubes and the bandages but an overwhelming sadness came over me in spite of all the love and support that was being sent my way. Sleep was very difficult and I found myself awake well into the morning hours. The nurse suggested I take something to make me sleep. When Krisi was born, I was given "something to make me sleep" and it reacted opposite in my body and charged me up instead. That was an awful experience that I did not want to repeat. The nurse explained to me that medications have changed so much in the last twenty five years that that medication was probably no longer in use. She suggested I try what they had as I really did need to get some rest. I finally agreed and was able to relax and sleep for a few hours.

Saturday, May 15, 2004
Day 27

HOSPITAL TIME MOVES on no matter how much sleep you've had the night before. It suddenly dawned on me that I had not taken a Prempro since the morning of the 13th. That was two days ago. Perhaps that was the cause of my anxiety. I talked it over with the nurse and she agreed with me that that would make me anxious. Hormone replacement does work in that way. She called my doctor and received permission to give me the Prempro. The morning passed rather quickly again between doctor visits, the nurse helping wash my hair with "Hair" a rinse free shampoo in a cap and Butch coming for a visit. In spite of my lack of sleep, I really felt pretty good. The doctor told me that I could go home if I wanted to. I was ready but a little concerned about the drain tubes and the pain pack that was installed. The pain pack was a bag of pain relief medication that fed directing into my incisions through a very tiny tube. I could control the amount that I wanted/needed. It was in a black bag with a strap over my shoulder. It didn't make moving any easier but certainly helped the pain. The pain pack was pulled which gave me a little more ease in movement—one less thing to worry about. Butch was trained in how to take care of the drain tubes. We were given pages of instructions and appointments along with bags of bandages and what not to keep me comfortable. We carefully left for home. *Wow what a beautiful day. I don't remember the weather outside—but inside the car it was warm and sunny. I had the surgery behind me. The cancer gone and I was on my way home to healing and hopefully health. I had certainly climbed the large mountain that was in my path from there to here! But I did hurt and I was pooped!*

I came home from the hospital early this afternoon with four drain tubes, hands full of pills to relieve the pain and stop infection, a box of rubber gloves for draining the tubes, bandages, ace wraps, even a product to dry wash my hair which is driving me nuts. Rita and Joe, Butch's sister and husband, had carried the recliner up from the family room into the living room and placed it in front of my bay window overlooking the driveway. What a perfect spot for me to watch the going and coming and to heal. I had Butch cover the chair with a quilt that my Grandmother from one side had sewn together the pattern and my Grandmother from the other side had put together with a backing and padding and then quilted for me. I felt in a sense wrapped in their love. I used bed pillows to prop up my arms and to keep handy in case I needed something to hug while I coughed or sneezed. Butch bought a new TV and wall mount for my healing corner. He plugged in a telephone within my reach and moved my CD player so that I could operate it with the remote control. I had my pills and water close at hand and a bathroom just a short walk done the hall. Talk about comfort and love! I was hurting but it felt so wonderful to be home and on the healing side of things. Talk about being spoiled! I am so blessed.

The delivery trucks kept coming all afternoon. We joked about them having an accident running into each other in the driveway. By evening, my living room was filled with beautiful arrangements and lovely plants. We had brought a car full home with us from the hospital as well. I told Butch that it smelled like a funeral home in our living room. He just laughed and told me that it was much better than a funeral home. He said, "You are alive and here to enjoy the plants and flowers. That seems much better to me!" He was right and enjoy I did. I pretty much spent my time listening to Don Moen's CD <u>God Will Make A Way</u> and sleeping and resting.

Butch became "nurse Butch" as he cared for me ever so gently and lovingly. Every few hours he had to drain and measure and record the fluid collecting in all four of my drains. He cooked and brought me food, made sure I had plenty of water and that I took my pills on time. He helped me wash up and settle into my chair for the evening. Krisi of course was at hand when Butch couldn't be there. She then took over the same duties.

It was the most comfortable for me in the recliner. The chair was a gift from my Dad to Butch for his service many years ago when my Mother had her mastectomy and needed to be taken daily for radiation treatments. Butch being in business for himself at the time had more flexibility in his schedule and was able to do that driving for her so my Dad didn't have to take off from work quite so much. How ironic that I was now using that same chair to bring me comfort after my own surgery of the same kind.

> *Thank you Lord for seeing me through my surgery*
> *and for sending "earth angels" in the form of Butch, Krisi*
> *and family and friends to care for me. I am very blessed*
> *and so very grateful. Amen*

Sunday, May 16, 2004

Day 28

EACH DAY I'M feeling better and stronger. I start out the night sleeping in our bed then about 2:30 a.m. or so I move downstairs to my recliner. I still find that to be most comfortable. It's easier to prop my arms up on the pillows when I'm half sitting up. We have a large security light that shines in the part of the lawn that I can see from my window. I do enjoy the view even in the wee hours of the morning when sleep will not come.

My brother and his wife from Oshkosh, WI., Dave and Faye, have been here all weekend. Faye is an R.N. so she has been relieving Butch of his nursing duties and helping me out a lot. It was good to have them here but they are heading home this afternoon. More visits from family and friends helped to pass the day. Our friend, Andy, from up at the lake, came to visit bringing gifts of homemade mushroom soup with sour cream, a bouquet of lily of the valley that he had picked for me, and a large trivet that he had made out of wine corks. He served me my soup right in my recliner and generally made me feel pretty special. The newlyweds, Carrie and Frank, even stopped in to wish me well. The telephone keeps ringing and best wishes keep pouring in. *I'm certainly not traveling this road alone by any means. What a blessing!*

Monday, May 17, 2004
Day 29

LAST NIGHT VICKI, one of my "Sisters in Spirit", brought dinner and helped me wash my hair again with that bed head stuff. *How wonderful to have friends that I feel so comfortable with and they with me that she can wash my hair and do such personal things for me. What a blessing to be sure.*

After she left, I decided to try a bath. Butch wanted to know if I felt I needed some help. Of course I was sure I could do it myself. I ran about an inch of hot soapy water into the tub and carefully crawled in. It felt so wonderful! I just sat there for a few minutes enjoying the healing power of water. When I started to try to wash myself, I realized that it was too painful to move my arms in such a way as needed to scrub my body. I called for Butch and found that he was waiting right outside the bathroom door knowing full well that I would not be successful in accomplishing my mission. He helped me out of the tub and had me sit on the edge. He gently and ever so carefully washed my back, neck and arms. "Did you ever think thirty some years ago when we got married that one day I'd be giving you a bath like this?" he laughed. I replied, "You mean me with this flat chest? I'm just glad that there is no hidden camera for Funniest Home Videos."

> *It felt rather strange to have Butch help me dry and dress and all but it was wonderful to feel clean and ever so loved. It was one of the tenderest moments of our marriage. I'm working very hard on being a "gracious receiver". It's not easy. For some reason, I have a hard time letting Butch and Krisi wait on me. I feel so bad that they have to do that stuff for me. I also know how helpless they feel with this whole thing and by helping me in this way it makes them feel better as well as me.*

We came downstairs armed with shampoo and a towel. Butch carefully washed my hair in the kitchen sink. He was so gentle and caring and it felt sooooooo good. I hate dirty hair!

I told Beth, my mother-in-law, that she should be so proud of her son and his care for me. She cried feeling as helpless as everyone else. She really didn't know how to react to the compliment. I guess she has a hard time being a gracious receiver as well as I do. I'm so glad to be on the healing side of surgery even if I am uncomfortable. A couple more days of drains should do it I hope. Maybe by Thursday the last two will be pulled. The mailbox is loaded daily with cards and letters of encouragement. *I didn't realize that I was so loved! The prayers, cards & letters, caring acts of kindness are certainly lifting me up and carrying me through this breast cancer journey. Thank God!*

Krisi came after school to "take care" of me. She changed the bedding, swept the floors, watered plants, folded clothes, shook rugs and who knows what all else. What a gift she has been all of her life and especially now. I was in the process of telling her it was time to go home and take care of her own husband when in he drove. They fixed brats on the grill for dinner. It was good for the four of us to have some quiet family time to discuss future options regarding our estate planning process.

Opposites

By Carolyn Salter

The dark side of the earth
Will soon be the bright side
Happiness of being together
Follows the poignancy
Of being apart.
Ups and downs
Positives, negatives
All in balance
Needing each to appreciate
The other

I've been doing a lot of complaining about the drain tubes. Butch asked me what they felt like. I told him it was like taking a broom handle and putting it behind your back and then draping your arms up and over the front of it on each side. THEN take two wooden pencils and shove them under your skin leaving about 2–3 inches protruding. Now move, and lie down, and stand up, and pee and wipe. I think I drew a pretty good picture for him.

I was hurting pretty good before bed tonight. About all I could do was cry and swallow pills. I cleaned up as best I could with such limited use of my arms and then lay down on the bed that looked so inviting. I slept until the news came on and then decided to get up and go shut off the computer. It was pretty well locked up. I had been online earlier viewing some pictures of the wedding that Frank and Carrie emailed me and Butch had tried to run a search that really took care of things. The date had even reset to January 1904! No way am I going back to that date! I'd much rather look ahead at this point. As the tears streamed down my face, I tried to type a command or two to get things straightened out. What a miserable mess! That is both me and the computer. Butch helped me to get things shut down and then helped me to go to "chair" instead of bed. My lazy boy with a couple of pillows under each arm is the BEST! Two pain pills and I was set. I slept very hard for about four hours. Of course by then I needed to use the bathroom as well as let Shady, our dog, out and in. Two more pain pills and the next thing I knew it was 6:00 a.m. *Thank God!*

Tuesday, May 18, 2004
Day 30

WE HAD AN appointment this morning with the plastic surgeon. He was able to take out two of the four drain tubes. Hurrah!!! I was a little nervous about that procedure and how much it would hurt. The doctor told me to lie down and take a deep breath. He asked me to take a second deep breath and pulled on the tube at the same time. Out it came. No problem. My concern was for nothing as I really didn't feel a thing. My underarms, however, are very sore from the drain sites. I think that hurts more than the actual incisions. I must have been doing some complaining as he told me that I needed to learn to walk before I could run and that it all takes time. That is just not part of my nature but I guess that is another lesson I need to learn. He taped me somewhat differently so hopefully my fat arms won't rub as much. It feels pretty tight but maybe that is a good thing. Butch took me home and headed for work.

Later in the afternoon he called to check on me and I told him I was going to walk out to the mailbox at the end of our driveway. He told me "no" that I had better stay close to my chair. "Remember you have to walk before you can run." *That's a tough one for me. Having people wait on me is another tough one. Today when we left the doctor's office I had a hard time opening the door. My chest pulls when I do things like that. I had to step aside and let Butch open the door for me. I do feel today like someone has been stomping on my chest. I guess I'll just give in and be lazy. Perhaps lazy is the wrong word to use.*

One Day At A Time

By Carolyn Salter

One step
Then another
Face it as it comes
Not before.
It may not come.

One step
Then another
Take each step
And live it
Love it
Use it
Fight the fight
Together
Live the love
Together
One step
Then another
One day at a time

Wednesday, May 19, 2004
Day 31

I'M STILL PRETTY much in misery with my arms. Butch called the doctor's office and talked to his assistant Barbara. She told us to come in to the office and she would pull the remaining two tubes. Oh happy day!!!!

Barbara and I had visited by telephone before the surgery. She's the one I asked to apologize to the plastic surgeon for my poor attitude and behavior. We talked at length that day about how I felt when I first consulted with the doctor. Barbara is a very empathetic, caring individual. She made me feel so comfortable and normal regarding my fears and anger. She assured me that they deal daily with patients facing cancer and understand the anger. We also talked about the word CANCER and what that means and how you feel when you first hear it used in connection with your own body. It is a terrifying experience. Today she explained to me that she did raise my concerns with the doctor reminding him that each patient is hearing this stuff for the first time not day in and day out as he does. She said that he told her that no one had ever said that to him before. *We all need reminders to be human now and again. As my outlook and attitude improve, so do my feelings regarding the plastic surgeon. He is treating me like a person not just another breast to reconstruct. He smiles and teases somewhat and seems much more approachable. He was probably that way all along. It was my attitude that needed adjusting. I wanted to be anywhere but at the beginning of a breast cancer journey.*

Barbara again was very thorough today in removing the last two tubes. She helped me breathe through as she pulled them out. It stung a little but I already feel better having them gone. She told me that I could SHOWER in the morning. She asked Butch to stand by outside while I do that as people that are weak sometimes get a little light headed. He told her he'd have no problem just getting right in with me. In fact, he thought perhaps he'd even take the dog in and we'd all get clean at once. We told her about Butch giving me a bath the other night and how we ended up laughing about it being a funniest home video. "I don't think so!," she replied. "It sounds very tender to me."

I had related the same incident earlier to a friend of mine from the seminary when she called to check on me. She said surely not funniest home video but a most tender loving moment. *I guess I'd have to agree. She said, "Your husband must love you very much." Again I have to agree. He has become quite a tender nurse. Who knew?*

Boy can I sleep! I load my Bose Music System with CDs, get comfy in my lazy boy and sleep and heal. The reoccurring theme of "slow and easy" recovery keeps coming back to me. Slow and easy does feel good. One card today talked about "the path of healing is an ever changing journey with threads of faith and courage softly intertwined among the gentle colors of hope". *I'm a believer. I'm so happy to be on this side of surgery. Tomorrow will be one week. I've come a long way and do plan to continue to rest and relax my way through this as much as possible.*

Tomorrow I see my original surgeon and Friday the oncologist. This has been a busy week what with all of the doctor appointments and the sleeping!?!?!?!

When Krisi was here yesterday, she asked me if I remembered the flowers in the pre-op room. She said they'd given me something to relax me and I kept saying, "It's not working. It's not working. I could get right up and walk out of here!" Then I asked them if they could see the beautiful flowers. I can just imagine the two of them grinning at each other over my head and snickering. Krisi said she asked me what kind of flowers they were and I told her, "Why pink azaleas!" Today when we got home from the doctor's office what was waiting by the door but a huge big beautiful pink azalea from some friends. Coincidence or have they heard the story?

My arms are feeling much better for sure. It will be good to remove the tape from under them in the shower in the morning if not before.

Friends have been showing up with dinner every night for us. What a thoughtful treat! It's great to have the food but even more enjoyable to have the friends stay and eat with us. Butch has made that rule: if you bring food you must stay and enjoy it with us. It has been great.

Thursday, May 20, 2004
Day 32

WE HAD AN appointment early this morning with the surgeon who did the mastectomy. All went very well. The pathology report confirmed that my lymph nodes were clear. *GOOD NEWS!* The doctor felt that I would not need chemotherapy but that he wanted me to visit with an oncologist anyway. Then he winked and told me to try and stay away from him. He said he really didn't want to see me in his office again. He chuckled through a good bye and good luck. I'm totally in the plastic surgeon's hands for the rest of my healing. We left the hospital and drove to Taylors Falls, MN to look at a tractor that Butch was interested in. I slept most of the way. It's great to have such a nice comfortable car.

Another good friend, Linda, came this afternoon and did my ironing. Bless her heart. *I even let her! Bless my heart. I'm learning. That is a big step for me in acceptance of my circumstances.* Two more friends showed up later, Nadine and Karen, with dinner. Butch saw all of the women here and adjourned to the shop to work on something. It's good for him to have a break from his nursing duties. I talked the girls into staying and eating with me. It wasn't very hard to convince them to stay. I was pretty tired by the time everyone left. But it was a good tired and a very good day!

Friday, May 21, 2004

Day 33

THIS AFTERNOON WE met with an oncologist at Lakeview Hospital in Stillwater. He was most kind and personable. We must have been there for almost two hours. We talked about me and my family history with cancer. He explained that I have an 8% chance of developing cancer somewhere else in my body in the next ten years. With chemotherapy, they could lower that to 6%. He felt that the side effects and risks of chemo, heart disease and leukemia, would be greater than the 2% increase in my chances of not developing more cancer. He recommended no chemo and no radiation. The tumors were well contained within the right breast and with no lymph node involvement. They were sure it had not moved. He also said that the taking of my left breast was a proactive way of preventing future breast cancer. Our plan is to watch everything careful by having a check up every four to six months or so, getting off the Prempro as well. *I can LIVE with that—literally.*

Dinner tonight with Jim and Brenda cooking was a celebration of no need for chemotherapy. *I am so very blessed.*

Look At Me Now

By Carolyn Salter from
Hurdles are for jumping

Look at me now
Isn't it great?
I've made it past
Cancer's own use by date!
I'm getting well
I'm winning through
Soon I'll be running
Whirling, dancing with you
Back into life
Back into swing
Nothing will stop me
I'll do everything.
Fear can't take hold
I'm being bold!
Look at me now!
Oh, Isn't it great?

Sunday, May 23, 2004
Day 35

TODAY IS BUTCH'S birthday. I have no gift and no cake and no party planned. I guess we've had other things on our mind!

Without the drain tubes, the fluid is really building in my chest. It feels very tight and painful to the point of not being able to breathe. I called the emergency number the plastic surgeon's office had given me and reached the Breast Care Center at Regions Hospital in St. Paul. She told me to come in to the ER and she'd see what she could do for me.

She calmed my fears as she explained that this fluid build up is very common. It is painful but it is not dangerous. Some women have to have the fluid aspirated three or four times before it stops collecting. It is part of the healing process. She also informed me that some of the women she has treated have been much fuller than I appear to me. Because I had the tissue expanders in, she was a little hesitant to try to aspirate any fluid for fear that she would accidentally puncture an expander. That would mean surgery again to replace the damaged expander. I encouraged her to try as the pressure seemed so great and I wanted some relief. It was extremely painful as she inserted the needle. In fact, I cried out and the tears began to flow. She immediately stopped and suggested that we wait for a radiologist to do an ultrasound so she would know for sure where the expanders were placed. She also reassured me that it was not life threatening – just uncomfortable. We decided to wait until Tuesday when I'd see the plastic surgeon again and let him draw off the fluid. She suggested warm showers and pain pills to get some relief now. *Tuesday feels like a long way away at this point in time. Please help me make it, Lord.*

Tuesday, May 25, 2004
Day 37

I GUESS I complained so much about the drain tubes that they perhaps removed them to quickly. I am retaining quite a bit of fluid around the tissue expanders. It feels very tight and painful. The plastic surgeon used a needle to aspirate the extra fluid and give me some relief. He didn't seem real concerned over the fluid. *Perhaps I'm just being a baby. I can't believe how tight and uncomfortable it feels.* He then began to fill the tissue expanders with saline solution. The valve in the expander was marked with a tiny magnet. The doctor used what looked like a miniature "stud finder". He ran that over my chest to locate the magnet and thus find the valve through which the Saline solution was added. My shape is beginning to grow! Pretty amazing stuff.

Bill and Phyllis, good friends of ours, brought dinner this evening. *We're going to be pretty spoiled soon when all of this food stops coming! We have some wonderful cooks for friends!*

Wednesday, May 26, 2004
Day 38

MY GRATITUDE GROUP came today and brought such joy. They cleaned my house from top to bottom, washed and ironed clothes, scrubbed floors, cleaned toilets. They brought plants and flowers for me to enjoy. On top of all that they served lunch and enjoyed it with me and left another meal for dinner that evening. I sat in my lazy boy and cried as I watched my friends cleaning and scrubbing for me. We laughed, cried, prayed, ate and enjoyed being together. It became a grateful celebration of my prognosis and eventual return to good health. *Gratitude in action! What more can I say? It was one of the most memorable days in my life. The feeling of being loved is all around me in the people that continue to minister to me and my daily needs.*

Thursday, May 27, 2004
Day 39

THE FLUID CONTINUES to gather around the expanders. It was beginning to feel tight again. I called the plastic surgeon's office and was told to come in and have one of his partners draw some off to give me relief. It worked. I wonder how long this will continue. *The drain tubes should have been left in longer I guess. That's my opinion— no one ever said that to me. The tubes were really uncomfortable and I'm glad they're gone. I'm wondering if I'm going to have to learn to live with this discomfort and tightness the rest of my life.*

Friday, May 28, 2004
Day 40

WE WERE PLANNING on heading to Rainy Lake today to open the cabin up for the season. Krisi and Jeff had both taken the day off of work to join us for the weekend. Butch was afraid that the trip would prove to be too much for me. He didn't think I'd be able to sit still and watch everyone else work and that I would over extend and put myself backwards on the healing. Instead we took a road trip to Wausaw and Waupaca, WI to look at a couple of tractors that Butch had found online. It turned out to be a fun day, a long drive, but fun. The tractor in Waupaca was what Butch was looking for so he made the deal and came home a pretty happy camper. I didn't do much but ride, eat and sleep. Krisi and Jeff joined us for the day. *It's always good to spend time together.*

Saturday, May 29, 2004
Day 41

YESTERDAY'S TRIP TIRED me out big time. I slept most of the day. The fluid is building again and getting tighter and tighter. They keep telling me this is normal. *I have to take their word for it. I don't like it. I feel like I'm carrying around something big and hard on my chest. My plastic surgeon tells me that I have a vivid imagination. He should try carrying it around for a while. I'm sounding a little crabby today.*

Sunday, May 30, 2004
Day 42

I DROVE MYSELF to church today. It was good to be back. I received lots of hugs and best wishes. I felt very loved and supported.

I'm getting pretty full of fluid again. *It feels like I have an inner tube around my chest and it is getter tighter and tighter. I'd like to make it until Tuesday's appointment rather than go to Regions Hospital ER on the weekend. I'm learning that the tightness is normal and not to worry about it just live with it.*

Monday, May 31, 2004
Day 43

THE WEATHER WAS pretty rainy and cold. Krisi and I went shopping in Woodbury for her birthday tomorrow. Casual Corner worked out well. We were headed to have our nails done but the places were all closed for the holiday. In spite of the rain and wind, Butch and Jeff burned a big pile of brush at the farm. We squeezed in a "hotdog burn" between the showers.

Tuesday, June 1, 2004
Day 44

I MADE THE holiday weekend without going to the ER to have fluid removed. Carole, my friend, drove me to the clinic today. I feel pretty good, a whole lot stronger. The plastic surgeon drew out more fluid from around both of the expanders. He then put more saline solution into the expanders on each side. My left breast is now 90% full. Next time he'll just put in a little more then we'll stop. I told him that for forty years I was big breasted and that I did not want that again. As he was filling my right breast like what seemed forever, I said, "Hey, remember I don't want to be a Dolly Parton!" He laughed and said that he was doing a little trick and drawing off some fluid. I was impressed. When he finished he told me that he felt perhaps my right expander was damaged from all of the aspirating of fluid. Which means it may have a hole in it. If so, it will need to be replaced in another forty-five minute surgery to remove the damaged expander and put in a new one. He had me feel how hard my right breast is now. He told me that if it gets soft and squishy in the next day or two that we do have a leak. If that's the case, I'm to call immediately and they will get things rolling for surgery so we don't delay the process too much. He was glad that I was feeling so positive about everything and hated to tell me that perhaps we were facing a little set back with a leak. I told him, "I'm this far now and not about to quit. I'll do what I need to do. I don't need chemo or radiation and the cancer is gone. What more can I ask for? If we need to replace the expander, then that's what we'll do. It's not the end of the world."

Carole and I went for coffee before coming home. We stopped at Valley Creek mall where I picked up two charms for Krisi's birthday today. We'll be celebrating at Wiederholt's Supper Club this evening. I'll try not to think about a possible leak.

Wednesday, June 2, 2004
Day 45

THE BIRTHDAY PARTY was fun last night. The food was great as well. Jeff gave Krisi a gold toe ring as a gift. Her Dad asked her, "What the hell is that for?" She just grinned and held the ring up to her nose and laughed. Butch responded, "Oh for crying out loud!" *We all laughed and it felt so good to feel so normal.* We saw another couple there having a quiet dinner compared to our noisy one. He also is dealing with cancer and not with the glad results that we are experiencing. But for the Grace of God go I. We didn't even talk about my squishy right expander.

Thursday, June 3, 2004
Day 45

I CALLED THE plastic surgeon's office today and talked to Barbara. I told her that my right expander had gotten soft. She wasn't surprised. We talked about scheduling surgery. Later in the afternoon she called back with surgery scheduled for Thursday, June 10 at 12:00 noon at Lakeview Hospital in Stillwater. I was to arrive at the hospital at 10:00 a.m. I was to come into the clinic on Tuesday, June 8 to see the plastic surgeon before surgery. Here we go again. My positive attitude was leaking into some anger.

Monday June 7, 2004
Day 50

I HAD ANOTHER pre-op physical today at the clinic in Stillwater. Some of the tests did not have to be repeated from my last pre-op since it was less than a month ago. That made me feel somewhat better.

Diane Davies

Tuesday, June 8, 2004
Day 51

ALL I DO is go to the doctor! Today it is back to the plastic surgeon's office. I wonder how the rest of the world is doing.

Thursday, June 10, 2004
Day 53

I NOW KNOW the routine. Going in this morning for surgery was certainly not as bad as a month ago. Some of the same people were working and were a little surprised to see me back so soon. This time I walked into surgery and got up on the table before they started to put me under. I really hadn't seen the operating room before. I was much more relaxed. All went well and by 4:00 p.m. I was home and back in my healing chair with pills for pain and pills to stop any infection. We were back to the drain tube routine as well. The healing should go faster this time.

Tuesday, June 15, 2004

Day 58

BACK TO THE clinic again today. During surgery, they started to put saline solution into the expander so that we didn't get too far behind. Healing happens and things look really good. I feel a lot of tightness in my breasts. (I'm beginning to feel like they belong to me and are a part of my body. I can't believe I just called them my breasts!) Sometimes it feels like I have on a new bra that is too tight and itchy and sore. Especially when I'm tired I get that feeling. I want to take the bra off and get some relief but it is inside me and cannot be removed. The best remedy is to lie down and stretch out. The plastic surgeon said that all looked great. He added more solution, removed the drain and told me to come back in a month.

Wednesday, June 16, 2004
Day 59

SHORTLY AFTER MY surgery Mickey O'Connor came to visit me. She brought with her a pink Beanie Baby named Hope to help with my healing. She also brought information on a breast cancer support group that meets in Hastings on the third Wednesday of each month at the Regina Care Center. Mickey and her friend, Claire Mathews, lead the group and invited me to join. This evening at 7:00 was the first meeting that I attended. The women there ranged in age from thirty two to ninety three all of whom had suffered with breast cancer at one point in time. Some were ten year survivors and some were longer and some were shorter. Some had finished treatment long ago and some were just starting. One gal had just had her surgery the day before I had mine. This was her first time attending as well. The women shared their stories with us and made us feel very welcome. We shared our stories and discussed the many differences and similarities that we found. I can see that we all have a lot to learn from each other and to share with each other and support each other which is the purpose of the group.

We talked, laughed, hugged and enjoyed each other's company. They have about thirty women on their membership list with about ten in attendance. I had no idea how prevalent this disease really is. I talked about my feeling that everyone was staring at my chest. Most of the women laughed and began to share with me their "staring at chest" stories. I left the meeting feeling like I belonged. I will return for the next month's meeting.

Friday, June 25, 2004

Day 68

TODAY'S CHECK UP was with my internist to see how I'm doing with the Paxil and without the Prempro and to check on my blood pressure. I'm experiencing some hot flashes and a few night sweats. That is what the antidepressant is supposed to be helping with now that the Prempro is gone. He wanted to know if the symptoms were unbearable or if I thought I could handle it. When I think about where I've been and how far I've come, I guess I can handle a few hot flashes! I really don't want to take any more pills than necessary. Another good report. We're moving along toward health.

I was complaining to my friend Carole that it seems like all I do is go to the doctor. She replied with a twinkle in her eye, "Well, Diane, don't you know that's what old people do with their time?" *I guess if the shoe fits, wear it! Right?*

June 25, 26, 27 & 28, 2004
Day 68, 69, 70 & 71

BUTCH'S SISTER RITA and her husband Joe, along with Joe's brother Mel and Mel's wife Julie, offered to help us open up the cabin for the summer this weekend. We all headed north to Rainy Lake and to our island "Campbellot". It felt so wonderful to be there again. We call it our little bit of heaven on earth. Earlier this spring, I wasn't so sure I'd ever see it again. Thanks to our visitors we accomplished the opening tasks and still had time for a little fun. *What would we do without friends?* I wasn't allowed to do much of anything. I'm going to be spoiled rotten before this cancer journey ends!

Wednesday, June 30, 2004
Day 73

I'M BECOMING MORE and more comfortable with my new body parts. Sometimes I forget all about them. I suppose it's like wearing braces on your teeth. They are uncomfortable at first but as time goes on you tend to forget about them and then they become the norm. Some days I wake up and get out of bed and feel like I'm carrying around a wooden shelf on my chest. My underarms feel better without the drains and all but they still rub on the fat or whatever I can feel there. The expanders are getting full and feel pretty hard to me. When I bump into something with my chest, it feels weird and pretty fake. I feel like I have a book strapped to my body and that is what I hit. When I give people hugs, my new breasts feel hard. *I wonder what they feel like to the person I'm hugging. No one has ever said anything about that, but then I guess they probably wouldn't. I'll have to ask someone sometime.*

> *Wow! It's the end of June. The time is going. Throughout all of this I've never had that "boobless" feeling. I'm glad that I could start reconstruction immediately and didn't have to experience that flat chestedness. I can look at my body in the mirror and*

I still have something there. The scars are a badge of courage that I wear proudly. I've even shown them off to my girlfriends occasionally. Most are eager to see and feel. Some turn away. When people ask, I'm eager to share as it helps me as well to talk about it and to be comfortable with it. Krisi was right so many months ago when she told me to come up with some smart remark to break the ice. I usually pull my shirt tight and say something about the new me. That gets people laughing and gives them permission to look and ask questions. Which they do. Men and women alike. Once that's over, we can get on with the conversation.

I'm beginning to feel more and more like being out and about with family and friends. Walks, lunch dates, a little shopping and cleaning house as well as cooking and baking fill my days. I'm so glad to be able to do those things once again.

July 2, 3, 4, 5, 2004
Day 74, 75, 76, 77

THE DENMARK TOWNSHIP Card Club, a group of our friends and neighbors that meets monthly to play cards and talk smart, went with us to Rainy Lake. It was a fun weekend as usual and it felt so good to be both back at the lake and out with friends – back to a more normal life. Of course, I wasn't allowed to do too much of anything in the way of work. What's wrong with that?

July. 9. 10. 11. 2004
Day 81, 82, 83

WE HAD THE Lindemann Family Reunion in Lady Smith, WI at Jason and Carie's lodge. With twenty one of us there, they had room for all. What an amazing place. We had a great time. Matching T shirts, fun and games, lots of good food. Who could ask for more? Some of women in the family wanted to have a peek at my new chest and others did not. I'm comfortable doing that as I do not really feel like it's me. It's recreated, and smaller, with scars running from under my arms to the middle of my chest on each side. It really doesn't look too bad.

Wednesday, July 14, 2004
Day 86

MY FIRST YEAR of college, I went to Mankato State where I made many wonderful friends. A group of us still get together for lunch now and then to get caught up with each other lives. Today we met at LeeAnn's in Hastings. The conversation of course eventually turned to breast cancer. They had many questions and many fears. We talked for a long time as I explained the procedure I was undergoing to have new breasts reconstructed. I finally asked if they would like to see. Right there in the kitchen I took off my blouse and continued the discussion using my body as a prop. One of the gals laughed and said, "Boy, you can never take the teacher out of Diane. Who else would turn this into a teachable moment?" Another remarked, "I think this is very helpful. Who knows maybe next week it will be you or I facing the same thing. It's good to know a little about this." It made me feel good to be able to share and perhaps in some way help someone else.

Tuesday, July 20, 2004
Day 93

TODAY'S FILL AT the plastic surgeon's I think will be my last. I'm comfortable with the size and feel pretty good about stopping. I've been wearing a sports bra that zips up the front on the advice of my doctor. He felt that the bra would help hold the expanders and push them more towards the front to give me more of a natural look and to help with the discomfort I still feel under my arms. He's right. It has done all of that.

He now wants me to go for a couple of months and in a sense "test ride" my new breasts. "Try on your clothes and see if you like the look and feel of the way they fit," he told me. He also explained that if I'm not happy, we can easily add more fluid or take some out depending on what I wanted. He gave me a thirty page document to read regarding silicone implants and assured me that at my next visit we would discuss the options thoroughly. He wants to wait now for the expanders to do their work and create a pocket for the implants. Then we'll talk about the next surgery.

It certainly feels great to be this far along. Some days I can forget all about it. Only when I take off my shirt am I reminded of my continuing journey. Some days are still uncomfortable physically. If I'm busy and don't think about it my new breasts feel fine. At other times, I can still feel "the book" I'm carryng out front. That usually happens when I'm tired. I've had a few opportunities to share personally with a couple of women facing breast cancer and surgery. I hope I have been as helpful to them as others were to me.

Wednesday, July 21, 2004
Day 94

I ATTENDED MY second breast cancer support meeting tonight. Many of the same women were there as last month. No one in the group had undergone breast reconstruction. In fact, one of the leaders said that only one other woman in the entire group had had reconstruction. They all wore prosthesis or nothing at all. They had many questions for me. After trying to answer their questions as best I could, I finally said, "Well would you like to see?" The leader answered for all when she said, "Oh I was hoping you would say that!" as she quickly jumped up and closed the door. Another one of the gals closed the drapes as she said, "People walking by might wonder what kind of a meeting we are having here." So we had a little show and tell time after which they had more questions. They were all very interested and very grateful for my willingness to share. *Perhaps in this way I may be helping other women make decisions about their own bodies.*

Tuesday, August 17, 2004
Day 119

ALL WENT WELL at the plastic surgeons today. The healing and the stretching are happening. We've stopped adding solution as I feel that I am as large as I would like to be. He reassured me that if I changed my mind, we could always add more. In fact, he also said that if I felt I was too large, solution could be removed. Now we need to wait a couple of months to let nature do its work and form the cavities for the implants. We discussed the pros and cons of saline solution implants and silicone implants. The saline implants, as I understand it, will feel somewhat harder than the silicone. If they would develop a leak, the saline solution would be absorbed easily by my body. The solution tends to evaporate slowly from the saline implants creating the need to replace them in ten to fifteen years. The silicone on the other hand will have a more natural feel. The silicone tends to adhere to itself. If a leak should develop, the silicone would tend to stay in the cavity created for the implant. Replacement of the silicone implants would be necessary between fifteen to twenty years. Because the silicone is not approved by the FDA, I would need to be a part of a five year study which means a yearly visit to the plastic surgeon. Not all surgeons and not all hospitals are approved to insert the silicone implants. My plastic surgeon can do the surgery but I would need to go to Regions Hospital in St. Paul rather than Lakeview in Stillwater. I would also have to be registered with the FDA so that they would know how to contact me in the case of a recall. *The more natural feel and the longer time frame before replacement helped me to decide to go with the silicone implants.* I made my decision and signed the necessary paperwork. *It seems like the decisions are getting easier.*

Wednesday, September 15, 2004
Day 148

THE SUPPORT GROUP met again tonight. Anne, the girl that had her initial surgery the day before I did, came this evening with a scarf over her head. Her hair is entirely gone from the chemo. She very bravely took off her scarf to show us her bald head. Her goal is to walk into a store without her scarf for the entire world to see. "Look at me. I'm fighting cancer. This is who I am like it or not!" is the message she wants to give. I told her that I had to stop at Walgreens on my way home and invited her to join me scarf less if she'd like. She declined my offer and said that she wasn't quite ready yet.

>*I look at Anne and once again realize how grateful I am. I could have been bald by this point and wearing a scarf as well if I would have needed chemotherapy. I admire her courage and strength. What a role model she is for her own daughter and family. Without coming to this support group, I never would have known Anne's story or the stories of all the other women that attend. Knowing them and their stories helps me to know myself better. I thank God for leading me in this direction. This*

support group thing works for me. I know there are many women out there who do not take advantage of this kind of assistance. I am grateful that it helps give me strength and that I perhaps can help others in the process.

Tuesday, September 21, 2004
Day 154

SEPTEMBER HAS BEEN such a busy month. First we went to Mount Pleasant, Iowa for a Steam Engine Show. Later in the month it was off to Reno for the National Air Races. And finally we headed to our cabin in Canada. Soon we'll be heading back out to the west coast to Sacramento for a family wedding then back to the cabin to close up for the winter. There just has not been time to schedule in my surgery to have the expanders removed and the implants inserted. I'm now scheduled for surgery on Friday, October 15, 2004. The original schedule was for a week earlier on October 8 but Dr. Mann will be out of town as he's going home for the Canadian Thanksgiving that weekend. His office called and rescheduled for the 15th. *I was bummed but what's another week after I've waited this long?*

I have a pre-op visit with the plastic surgeon this morning at 8:20 then a few weeks to wait and we're home free. Yeah! A little more healing to do and this ordeal is over. Hurrah!

What a disappointing visit that turned out to be! The doctor came in and did his usual exam. We talked about nipple creation. I asked if that happened at this next surgery. He explained that the nipple creation and the tattooing were two separate procedures that would happen down the road a bit yet. That was news to me. I figured this would be the end. He then asked, "Well, what's the plan?"

I said, "What do you mean what's the plan? I'm scheduled to have my implants inserted on October 15. Don't tell me you're going to postpone again? Won't you be back in town then from your vacation?"

He replied, "Hasn't anyone called you?" He then went on to explain that he was now on probation and would not be able to put in my implants until further notice. I was pretty much blown away. No questions or comments came to my mind. I must have been in a state of shock. His assistant, Joan, told me that it was a paper work mix up and that it would be straightened out soon. She suggested I just be patient and wait for the doctor to do the surgery as I would be more pleased with the outcome. I left the office totally confused and frustrated. I called Butch from my car and he reminded me that I have every right to have all of my questions answered. He suggested that I call the office again when I get home and find out just exactly what is going on and when do they feel the surgery could be scheduled.

We have a neighbor who is a plastic surgeon in Minneapolis. I decided to give him a call to find out just what he knew about this probation business. His wife said she would contact him and have him get back to me. By now, I had quite a few questions on my to find out list. *I was beginning to question the integrity and credibility of the plastic surgeon that had been chosen. What's a person to do when you are half way through the reconstruction process and suddenly your plan no longer exists?*

I called Joan again at the plastic surgeon's office and she reassured me that this probation had nothing to do with his credibility. She explained to me that because I had chosen to have silicone implants an extra amount of paperwork was required as the silicone is not approved by the FDA. I knew this as I had been given about 30 pages of information to read and sign discussing the risks and all and agreeing to be a part of a five year study because of the silicone.

She explained that that was only part of the paperwork. The Dr. had more forms to fill out as well as the facility where the surgery would be performed. The mix up with one of more of these forms was not on my case but with another patient of the doctor. When this happens, the doctor is put on what they call probation until the paperwork is straightened out. No other implants can be put in until the probation is lifted. She assured me that everything possible was being done to get this problem taken care of. She felt confident that I would have my surgery on the 15th of October. She promised to call me as soon as she had any news either way.

Later on in the evening our neighbor returned my call. He had talked to my plastic surgeon's office and had been given pretty much the same information as I had been told. He assured me that what I had been told was truthful and that was actually how the system worked when it came to silicone implants. He also helped to relieve my growing anxiety over the capability of my doctor. He said that he had an excellent reputation and was a fine surgeon. He also offered to do the surgery for me if mine was not able to get the problem straightened out. We laughed about how we could meet at the mailbox for my exams. I could just lift my top and he could do the exams under the bright blue sky and the peering eyes of the entire neighborhood. In all seriousness, he felt that it would be best for me to finish up the reconstruction with my original surgeon as he was very capable and had started the procedure and knew me and my circumstances. He assured me that it would all get done perhaps not within my time frame but that it would happen.

I continue to ask why this all has to be so difficult. I run and run and then hit another cement wall. I really have tried so hard to keep up with a positive attitude and a sense of humor throughout. It is difficult to understand. However, as Joe said, it will all happen. Perhaps just not in my time frame. I continue to struggle with my impatience. God in his wisdom must have this lesson for me to learn regarding patience. When I prayed for patience a number of years ago, I found myself teaching first grade. Now that truly is a lesson in practicing being patient. There is a difference, however, in being patient with children and being patient within my own life. I continue to learn and grow.

When I think about this nipple business; I ask myself what do I really need them for? If I have them created, I'll just have to wear clothing that will help to cover them up so they don't show. Why do I even want them? Why don't I just stop at the end of this next surgery? Do I need the tattooing? I don't think so! When discussing this issue with my doctor, he asked me about Krisi and was sure that being a young woman of the 2000s that surely she had a tattoo. I guess he doesn't know Krisi very well! Once again I ask, 'Why do I need that? I really don't plan on being a topless waitress or anything at this stage in my life. And I don't make it a habit of running around nude? Butch tells me that it's my body and I need to decide what I want and don't want. Another decision to make. At this point in time, I'm thinking NO to both the nipples and the tattooing. I have time to make my final decision one of these days.

Thursday, September 23, 2004
Day 156

JOAN FROM THE plastic surgeon's office called today to tell me that all was taken care of and that my surgery would go on as scheduled on October 15. She explained that I would receive a mailing with information from Regions Hospital along with a post-op appointment date with the doctor. That information would arrive in a day or two. *I'm a happy camper once again.*

I wonder why all the bumps are put in the road? Why can't things go smoothly as planned? Why did I have to endure two more days of frustration before the crooked road was made straight once again? I thank God for the good news of surgery being back on schedule. Now it's on to Sacramento and then closing up the cabin.

Wednesday, October 13, 2004
Day 176

THE TRIP TO California and the wedding all went well. It was especially warm. I expected somewhat cooler temperatures in October. High 80s low 90's are not my cup of tea. The week in Canada was spectacular. Much cooler temperatures, bright sunshine, and beautiful fall foliage. We visited with many friends and buttoned up the cabin for the winter. We came home on Monday so that I could get ready for my surgery on Friday. Today I have my pre-op physical with my internist. I could not get in to see him in Stillwater until after the 15th of October but he had an opening today at his Somerset, WI office. It was a beautiful day for a drive along the river. Once again I enjoyed God's creation in full fall color.

My physical went well and I even received a flu shot in spite of the shortage of serum this season. I guess that is one advantage to having been diagnosed with cancer this spring. As I was about to leave, my internist told me that I really looked good. He explained that he felt that I really looked at peace. He quickly added that he didn't mean that I was off the wall before but that I now seemed so calm and at ease with this whole thing. I agreed that I did feel that way and contributed the feeling to all of the love and support that I had been given by my family and friends. He especially asked about Butch and wondered how he was doing with the changes in my body and in our life. I told him how lucky and blessed I was in that Butch has been my strength. That he is the one that keeps me grounded and gives me a reality check when needed. He then explained that not all husbands handle it that well and reassured me that I indeed was fortunate. We talked about the nipple and tattooing issue as well. He reassured me once again that the decision is totally mine. In a sense, he gave me permission to stop the reconstruction procedure at the point that I'm comfortable. "Don't be forced into anything that you do not want." *I appreciate his most caring advice. With that physical behind me, the next and hopefully final step is the surgery on Friday.*

I found this poem from Carolyn Salter that puts into words what Butch has said to me through his words, actions, and love.

Hey Babe

By Carolyn Salter

Hey Babe, you're still the one
Cancer doesn't kill off love you know.
And while you don't like your body
I still do.
Even the missing bits
It's all part of you.

Look beyond the physical
Do you think that's all I find?
Look beyond the skin deep
Go into your mind
(It's a great place to be)
There's a whole sea of knowledge there
So don't despair.
Just because we can't do
All we once could
You're still the one for me
Doing me good.

Isn't that weird
I'm learning more from you
Than the other way round.
You're my support.

And I'm glad I've got you, Babe
So glad I've got you, Babe
And my love abounds.

Friday, October 15, 2004
Day 178

THE DAY IS rainy and chilly. I guess it's a good day for surgery. A nice long nap this afternoon in my lazy boy with my favorite quilt and afghan will be just the ticket. We arrived at the hospital at my appointed time, 8:45 a.m. I guess it was more like 9:00a.m after we drove around the parking ramp at Regions a few times trying to figure out just where to park. No food or drink since midnight last night finds my stomach growling a bit. *I feel pretty calm. Knowing that this is my last big procedure makes me feel good.* We check it at the desk. Butch is given a pager with the instructions that when the doctor is finished and will consult with him, the lights will blink. My name is called and in we go to get ready. I'm instructed to put on my gown, long white stockings to prevent blood clots and fancy little paper booties that I can't get to stay on my feet. The nurses come in to get my legs wrapped up in funny looking moon boots that go to my knees. Hanging from the bottom of the boots are plug ins of some sort. Another blood clot prevention device the nurse tells me. She also gives me "booty putting on 101", as she quickly puts my feet correctly into the slippers. The next step was the IV. The first attempt in the left arm left me with a real burning feeling as well as swelling and stiffness in my thumb. That one came out quickly with a second try in right hand that was successful. Now that I'm all hooked up, I need to go to the bathroom of course. So IV bag and all, off I waddle to the restroom down the hall. Once back in bed, I'm visited by all members of the surgical team. The plastic surgeon draws on my expanded chest all kinds of artwork. Papers are signed and we're ready to go. They come in to tell me that the schedule has been changed from 11:30 to 10:15 a.m. *That is fine with me. I'm ready to go. Let's get this over with.* I can see the team standing around out in the hall waiting for the surgical room to be ready. It's now 10:17 a.m. Then 10:20 a.m.. Finally the surgeon comes in with his surgical hat pushed up funny. He has a strange look on his face and my first reaction is, "Oh no! Don't tell me this is not going to happen?"

"That's right!" he replies. "Your implants are in Indianapolis and will not be here today."

"Shit!" was the first expletive out of my mouth.

He went on to explain that "she", whoever she may be, checked the schedule and saw that the surgery for October 8 had been canceled. Not looking ahead to see if it had been rescheduled, "she" sent the implants back to Mentor the company where they are made. Then he looked at me and said, "Why did you cancel for October 8?"

My reply, "I didn't! You did. You were going out of town. Remember? So what happens now? When can we reschedule? When will the implants get here?" as my questions went on and on.

He explained that Valerie, his secretary, was working on that right now and would probably have an answer for me before we left the hospital. He walked out of the room shortly thereafter. *I'm sure that some where in the conversation he said he was sorry but that does not come to my mind.*

Butch and I both looked at each pretty dumbfounded. "Now what do I do?" I said as I pushed the button for the nurse. An aide came in to see what I needed. I told her I needed to go home so please get someone in here to unhook me. The nurse arrived just as my tears started to flow. She comforted me as best she could and apologized for the mix up. She removed the IV and suggested I take the stockings and boots home and bring them back when the surgery was rescheduled. Butch looked at me pretty incredulously and we pretty much in unison said, "No way! We're not hauling that stuff around. Just throw it away." I dressed in a daze and we walked out of the surgery center. Butch dropped his pager at the desk and we headed silently for home. There didn't seem to be anything to say but, "Can you believe this?" *Another cement wall and this felt like a pretty big one to me.*

After arriving home, the list of questions began to grow again. I called the surgeon's office where Joan answered and apologized several times. She explained that someone at the hospital had sent the implants back to the manufacturer after seeing that the surgery on October 8 had been canceled. "We don't make these kinds of mistakes often, but when they happen it seems like they happen again and again to the same patient," she offered. I was not comforted. She also went on to say that she thought perhaps early November would be the first time the schedule would allow another surgery. I did not agree with her. She suggested I talk to Valerie as she's responsible for the scheduling. Valerie apologized at least three times as well and went on to tell me that we were scheduled for Thursday the 21st. "Of November?" I snapped. She calmly set me straight and replied, "No, that's next week Thursday at 7:30 in the morning. I did some juggling around and was able to get you in then at the earliest. We'll update your pre-op physical when you arrive at the hospital." "Thank you!" was about all I could manage to respond.

I then sent off the following email to family and friends and hit the couch where I slept for the rest of the afternoon:

"Family & Friends

It is October 15, 2004. A little after 12:00 p.m. I'm home from the hospital as my surgery did not happen today. (I'm a little angry—maybe a whole lot angry is better wording.) I arrived at the hospital at my appointed time. We did all the pre-op stuff including starting the IV (twice - once in each arm!?!?!?). I had talked to everyone I needed to talk to including the surgeon. He marked me all up with his black pen, signed and initialed me and we were just ready to go into the operating room when he came back in to my room and told me that the implants were not there. They had arrived on Tuesday and had been sent back to the company because my surgery on October 8 had been canceled. No one bothered to check to see if it had been rescheduled. So we wasted a lot of time for a lot of people for nothing. So rather fuming, I dressed and we left. Butch was not a very happy camper either. Now that I've finally had something to eat, I feel a little better. After calling the plastic surgeon's office, I'm rescheduled for Thursday, Oct. 21 at 7:30 in the morning. All I can say is it better work this time or I'll… or I'll what? What choice do I have at this point? I'm sorry to say I cried and hollered a bit but no implants no surgery. And we trust our lives to the medical system? I wonder! God in His wisdom must have a reason for all of this—but I'll be damned if I can figure it out right now. Thanks for listening. Keep those prayers coming as I'm losing patience."

I still cannot believe it. I figured by now I'd be finished and recovering. I'm angry to say the least but what can I do about it? Not much. I still need to have these expanders removed and the implant put in. I can not do it myself. No one said it would be easy but no one said it would be this frustrating either. Valerie in our conversation earlier said, "Well at least they hadn't put you out yet!" I didn't find that very comforting either or funny at this point in time.

Now my schedule is all goofed up. At least I can still host the seminar on Wednesday for my students. I may need to reschedule some of their observations however, depending on my recovery. It will all work out but why do I have to make all of the concessions? I guess I'm feeling pretty sorry for Diane right now. I need to remember that things could always be worse. I am still thankful that I did not need to undergo chemo or radiation. I am still thankful that the cancer is now gone from my body. I am still thankful that I have many years of living to look forward to. I am still thankful that I have the support and love of family and friends holding me up through all of this. I just need to continue to work on being patient and resign myself to the fact that I am not in control of these circumstances but I am in control of my reaction to it. I'll keep working on that with God's help.

Sunday, October 17, 2004
Day 180

I DECIDED THAT today in church I would make an announcement about my "surgery that didn't happen." That way I'd only have to tell the story once and would have fewer questions after the service. So I stood up at the appointed time and told my tale. I said that I wouldn't say what I said when the surgeon came in to tell me that the surgery would not happen today. Obid, our pastor, was quick to say, "What DID you say Diane?" I waited a few seconds weighing it over in my mind and then I shouted, "Shit!" The congregation laughed and broke into applause. *The hugs, kisses and best wishes I received after the service was heartwarming and overwhelming. What do people do without such a community to support them?* My daughter looked at me astonished and said, "I cannot believe you said "shit" in church!" Then she grinned.

Hopefully my sense of humor about this whole thing is returning. I'm still a bit put out about not being called before arriving at the hospital, however, it is a human institution and therefore mistakes must be expected. I just don't like expecting them to happen to me. Wes, a friend from church, suggested "Why not try an old pair of socks rolled up - who needs silicone?" *My outlook is better now and I pray for forgiveness of my anger. I still do feel that it was justified anger, however. Laughing about the whole mess feels better than crying about it. Now I need to get refocused for surgery on Thursday. I don't plan to leave for the hospital until I know that the implants are there waiting.* Another friend quipped, "They just don't have extra boobs laying around , huh?" *I guess they don't!*

Monday, October 18, 2004
Day 181

TODAY'S ONLINE DEVOTIONAL (daily-devotional@bbs. upperroom.org) used this Bible verse as it's basis; "Forgetting what is behind and straining toward what is ahead, I press on toward the goal to win the prize for which God has called me heavenward in Christ Jesus." Philippians 3:13–14 The mediation talked about Joseph who had many hurts in his life to remember. His brother's threw him in a pit and sold him into slavery. He was slandered by a beautiful woman and thrown into prison. Yet when he came into a position of power in Egypt, he forgave his brothers and he named his son Manasseh which means "God has caused me to forget" (Genesis 41:51). Joseph shows us how to move forward and forget the hurts of the past.

> *This "forgive and forget" theme of today's devotional and the many emails that I've received the last few days, is certainly my lesson to be learned. Where will it get me to nurse insults and injuries? I have come too far in this battle and have been way too successful to add hard feelings to it now. Help me Lord to leave past hurts behind and forgive those who have hurt me.*

Email responses regarding my lack of surgery:

"Look at your surgery (or lack of in your case) this way. Most people are mad and upset when they have to have surgery and you got to get mad and upset WHEN YOU DIDN'T HAVE SURGERY. Always have to be different don't you. All joking aside, I hope everything goes OK for you. Once again, I will think positive and talk to the guy above for a safe and speedy recovery. Take care."

"I can only imagine how distressed you must feel, after all of your emotional and physical preparation for surgery! Maybe, though, God has another plan, and that by delaying the surgery, you will have a better outcome. Maybe, the implants that were sent back were defective, or your surgeon wasn't at his best that day, or... You'll probably never know, but a week isn't too long to wait. You've already done the hard part—the diagnosis and surgery for cancer- so I know, and God knows, that you can get through this too, with your usual grace and humor!! My prayers are with you throughout this ordeal! (Don't be angry at my "silver lining" interpretation of this set back! I'd be just plain mad!)"

"I'm so sorry Diane. I'm with you, screw the medical system. They have me pretty messed up also & I'm more then pissed. I guess we just pray."

"Sorry to hear no new boobs and will keep you in my prayers. I think of you often and all that you've been through and wonder if I could do the same. Good luck on the 21st."

"My heart goes out to you... what a disappointment. I was angry just reading your note. You're right, there was nothing else to do... but the physical and probably more so, the emotional drain had to be tough. Our prayers continue for you with a special one on the 21st. Maybe in God's wisdom... they say not to have surgery on a Friday... who knows. God speed and will see you soon!"

"What a bummer!!!! I don't know what else to say!"

I can not dwell on the pain and hurt and frustration
of last Friday. It is over and done. The implants were

not there so they could not be put into my body. That will happen on next Thursday. I can fume and fuss and create a big stink and it will get me nowhere but upset, uptight, and angry. Is that how I want to live? By letting go of the anger now, I will be more stress free and relaxed when Thursday comes and the surgery does happen. I don't want to be the "bitch" they have to do the surgery on today. God in His way is showing me the path to follow. Forgive, forget, accept -will make for a happier me in the long run. Thank you Lord for showing me the way.

Tuesday, October 19, 2004

Day 182

I CALLED THE plastic surgeon's secretary this morning and my IMPLANTS ARE IN!!! We are a go for Thursday the twenty first in the morning at Regions. I asked her if she wanted me to come and hold on to them in my hot little hands until surgery. She didn't laugh but assured me that they would be safe and available on that morning. She explained that the person responsible for the mix up in sending them back really felt bad and was so sorry. *I was really trying to be funny but I guess my comment was not taken that way. I do believe that there were more people upset about last week than just me. I'll have to make my forgiveness known.*

Isaiah 40:31 was the online reading for today. "Those who wait for the LORD shall renew their strength. *Yes, waiting has been the most difficult part of this whole experience. First it was waiting for test results, then waiting to see the surgeon, then waiting for the day of the surgery, then waiting for healing and expanding, then waiting for the implants, then waiting for surgery again. It certainly has been a lesson in developing patience. Once again the devotional seems to have been written for me. "Life would be much easier if God acted according to our timetable!" And then: "If I never had to wait, I would have no need for hope in God and I would say fewer prayers for God's guidance." Another lesson for Diane to learn. My experience has taught me many things; The grass is greener, the sky bluer, my love for Butch stronger and more secure, family and friends DO love and support me, there is life after breast cancer, I'm so blessed not to have had chemo or radiation. I have a very wise and beautiful daughter who loves me very much, "I have learned about God's faithfulness and found strength for the next challenge in my life. I began to trust God's decisions and timing. I also learned that I do not always have the right answers and that God's ideas are better than I could ever imagine," teaches the author of today's devotional. My surgery will be Thursday! I wonder what surprises and exciting challenges lay ahead for me!*

Wednesday, October 20, 2004
Day 183

THE MANY ANGELS in our day to day life was the theme of the devotional that I read today. I looked up angel in my dictionary and was not surprised to find the meaning to be "a messenger from God". How many of "God's Messengers" have been active in my life as a result of this cancer? When I stop to think about it, I am truly amazed. God's Messengers in the form of family and friends have brought me words of comfort or challenge just when I needed them most. God's Messengers have brought blessings through family and friends, through phone calls, through emails, through health care providers, through members of our congregation, through students at the seminary, and even through strangers. God's angels are all around me! It is my job to have an open mind and heart to be willing to look for them each and every day. They are there!

Reading shared at the breast cancer support group;

Hope

Hope is not just one single quality or promise. Hope has to do with believing beyond today. Hope encourages me to follow my dreams, to believe in the part of me that envisions my wholeness. Hope is trusting that what is happening will eventually make sense, or if it never does, it will still offer an opportunity for growth. Hope assures me each morning that my life is of value no matter how unsettling or disturbing my current situation is. Hope encourages my heart not to give up and nudges me when it's time to move on. Hope doesn't need words or proofs or conditions. Hope accepts mystery and offers the gift of solid trust in the unknown. Hope doesn't pretend that I'll get all I want nor does hope deny that there will still be struggles down the road. Hope tucks promises of growth and truth inside the pockets of my struggles. As I look at my journey, I realize I would never be who I am and where I am today if it had not been for hope. Today, I will let hope have a permanent home in my life.

Author Unknown

Thursday, October 21, 2004
Day 185

I'VE BEEN ASSURED the implants are at the hospital and waiting for me. *I hope so. I don't want a repeat of the last time.*

A young cancer patient talks about her despair over her hair falling out in today's devotional. She realizes that no matter how small or big the problem, God cares and will help. *Once again written just for me wouldn't you say? Trust God with the details. Okay God, here we go.* Butch and I arrived at the hospital at our appointed time. The nurse that called me in reassured me once again that the implants were there and ready. They updated my pre-op physical as promised and I was ready to go. The gal who had mistakenly sent the implants back a week ago had called me yesterday to apologize. She also told me that she would be in to visit me before my surgery. *I was a little nervous about that visit as I wasn't sure how Butch would react to her. His anger had pretty much matched mine a week ago.* She was nervous when she arrived. She explained once again what had happened and apologized once more, maybe even twice more. She squeezed my hand and wished me luck and was gone. *That took courage. I admire her for owning up to a mistake and then doing something about it. Butch never said a word. He just smiled at me when she left.* Before taking me to surgery, the nurse gave Butch a voucher for the dining room so he could go and have breakfast while he waited. *I thought that was a little odd. It had never happened before.*

The next thing I remember is waking up in recovery. The man next to me was coughing and keeping me awake and all I wanted to do was sleep. The drain tubes were back but this time only one on each side. I knew the drill and I knew that we could handle it. It took a while for me to become fully awake. I remember having to move into a wheel chair and sitting there for a while while that awful coughing continued. Finally the nurse wheeled me back into another area where Butch was waiting for me. There was also a bouquet of flowers on the window sill. I thought that was a little strange as recovery does not usually allow such a thing. In the bouquet, was a free parking pass for the ramp. Butch and I laughed about how he should pull it out and stick it in his pocket. We didn't realize that it was meant for us to use. The nurse came in with water for me and told me to just rest and relax as long as I wanted. "When you feel ready, you can get dressed and I'll deliver you to your car. Take your time. There's no hurry." She was in and out several times and offered me something to eat. Butch helped me to struggle into my clothes. This time I remembered to wear something big and baggy that zipped up the front. As the nurse wheeled me out, she handed me the flowers and told me they were a gift from the hospital. *(Perhaps a little guilt on their part? Forgive and forget—right?)* I said my thank yous and we headed for home. Back to the lazy boy and the pillows and the drains and the pain pills and the healing.

October, 22, 23, 24, 2004
Days 186–188

REST AND HEAL. Heal and rest. I've been here before. This time is easier for sure. Certainly not the trauma of the first time around. The drains are uncomfortable but so is the tightness of the collecting fluid without them. I have my own little healing corner back and am doing well. The implants already feel softer that the expanders.

On Sunday evening, Krisi & Jeff were here watching TV with us. I stood up to go to the bathroom and left a smear of blood on the white leather sofa that I didn't know about. I undid my shirt and discovered that the tube on my left side had slipped out about five inches. I knew that it wasn't going to work to try and push it back it that far. I called Butch to come and help me. He was waiting for me to call as he had noticed the blood on the sofa. I asked him what he thought and he suggested that we pull it out the rest of the way. "It's up to you, Diane. I'll do whatever you want." I told him to go ahead and pull it out. I braced for the sting. Surprisingly it slipped right out. There was only about and inch of the tube left in. That was why the bloody mess on the sofa. Once we pulled it out, it was fine. No bleeding or leaking or anything. Krisi was probably the most upset as she had not been around too much before for the drain extravaganza. She thought perhaps we should go to the ER. Tuesday's doctor appointment was soon enough.

Monday, October 25, 2004
Day 189

I'm truly beginning to feel like my endurance of this cancer storm is coming to an end. It is not easy in the middle of the stormy tribulations to hang on to God and ride it out. "Why" is a word that keeps coming to mind. Why me? Why now? Why was my storm, compared to others around me, an easier storm? Life is good and so is God. I'll probably never have the "whys" answered. I'm so grateful to be where I am. My post-op visit is tomorrow. Doesn't that sound great – POST-OP? Thanks be to God.

BUTCH WOKE ME up this morning about 7:30 a.m.. With the drain tubes and all, I've been having some difficulty sleeping. I'm a side sleeper and the tubes under my arms make that a little uncomfortable. He was waiting for me to call Barbara at the plastic surgery clinic to see what time she wanted me to come in. After my splash bath, I gave her a call. She was just ready to call me to see how Sunday had gone. I explained to her about the left tube having fallen out. After a bit of discussion, I decided to go in this morning and have her pull the other tube as well. Then I'd keep my appointment tomorrow morning with the plastic surgeon for my post-op visit. I told her that my left breast was making funny noises. "Oh you have the squishies!" she giggled and explained that that too shall pass. It is the implants settling in to new surroundings. *Talk about gross!!!! I've certainly passed breast cancer/reconstruction 101! What a lot to learn and experience!*

Barbara was pleased with the way everything looked when I arrived at the clinic. She told me that they call the plastic surgeon "Dr. Breast" as he does such an excellent job of creating a good looking set of them. *I must admit, they do look pretty nice. A whole lot smaller than my original home grown variety!!! That is Good!* I'm a little bruised from the lipo suction I had done under my arms. (*Can you believe I agreed to that? Me, the one who hated everything about plastic surgery including the word PLASTIC!?!)* Well it does feel better and the "knots" under my arms are gone. *Another lesson learned: Sometimes I do have to listen to what other people tell me. I do not have all the answers even if I would like to think that I do.*

> *The day went well. It feels so good to have no tubes, no bandages, no knots under the arms. Butch was concerned that I'd do too much today. I didn't get done half of what I wanted to do. I just finished taking a WONDERFUL shower. The first one since surgery last Thursday. It's amazing how great hot water and soap feels. The implants are already much softer than the expanders ever were. I hope that stays that way. Butch said that the plastic surgeon told him that hardness was a sign of infection and that would mean more surgery. Let's hope that doesn't happen.*

Tuesday, October 26, 2004
Day 190

I HAD MY post-op appointment with "Dr. Breast" this morning. Barbara assisted him. We explained about the left drain tube coming out on its own. He explained that he had not stitched it in as he had done before and that then they sometimes do fall out. He was not at all concerned. He removed the lipo suction stitches and wanted to know if we had accomplished all in surgery that I wanted done. We discussed a little that my left breast appears a little lower than the right. He assured me that we could fix that fairly easily down the road. We also talked about the softness of the implants compared to the expanders. He explained that they should stay this way but that we wouldn't really know for about six months. My body needs to react to the implants and we have no way of knowing what that reaction may be. It may choose to make a capsule of hard scar tissue around it or it may not. Time will tell. If the scar tissue forms, there is a surgical procedure to help break up the scars and soften the appearance. "Hopefully that will not happen. And if it does, we'll talk about it then," was his reply. My next appointment is three weeks from now. He encouraged me to return to normal activity but to not take part in sports, jogging, aerobics etc. for a few weeks. I agreed that that would be real easy for me to give up!!!

As he was leaving the room, I told him that I was planning on writing a book about my breast cancer journey. He came back in grinning as I assured him that he would be a part of it. "The final chapter isn't written yet," he cautioned. *See, I do need to continue my work on patience. He has been a constant reminder to me to slow down and take one step at a time. I'm trying. I always want to get from "there to here" yesterday. It feels so good to be on this side of things. I know that I'm not finished with this journey but it feels good to celebrate the place I'm at today. And I think that is okay! A speaker I attended today said that before you can do anything you have to get up. If you stumble, get up again. Keep getting up until you accomplish whatever it is you set out to do. The next step is to be grateful for steps taken and to express that gratitude. Thank you Lord that I am this far on my journey. Be with me as I continue on. Amen*

Friday, October 29, 2004
Day 193

I've had a pretty busy week with student teachers and meetings and so forth. It does feel good to be home today with nothing on my agenda. I'm learning that there is nothing wrong with taking a good nap now and then and that's exactly what I have planned for this afternoon. I'm reading a good book. Talk about a perfect recipe: 1 good book, 1 comfy sofa, 1 fluffy pillow, 1 soft afghan. Add to that 1 tired body. Mix together for at least three hours and Viola! A little RR for Diane.

SOMETIME THROUGHOUT THIS journey, I've misplaced a favorite tablecloth. In an effort to find it, I cleaned (and I mean cleaned) two closets today with no luck. As I was finishing up and putting things away, I started with a little itching around my new implants. I put on a little Neosporin and tried to forget about it. We had dinner out with Grandma, Krisi & Jeff and as the dinner continued, so did the itching. It was driving me pretty much wild by the time we got home. I added more cream and tried to sleep. After finishing up reading my novel at about 1:30 a.m., I tried the sleep thing again and was at last successful. *Of course my mind is running away with things and all sorts of bad scenarios arise. What if I'm allergic to the silicone and the implants need to be removed? What if there is a silicone leak and that is what is causing the itching? What if… What if… What if… You know how the brain works at 3:00 in the morning!*

Saturday, October 30, 2004
Day 194

THE ITCHING CONTINUED throughout the night. With nothing again on my agenda, I decided to sleep as long as possible. The old brain kicks in about 8:30 a.m. with some more of those What ifs…

I decided to call the emergency number at Regions to get some advice. Before calling, I took a good look at my chest. The red itching spots followed straight lines along the incisions. It looks to me like I'm having an allergic reaction to the adhesive used in the bandaging. I still called to find out what to do with all this itching. I talked to the on call physician. He recommended that I use a hydrocortisone cream and rub it well and take Benedryl. He also suggested that I get in to see my plastic surgeon this week if at all possible just because that would probably make me feel better. He assured me that if I was having a reaction to the implants there would be fever and redness not just following the adhesive line. *That made me much more comfortable. I followed his advice throughout the day and did find some relief.*

> *As a patient, I have learned that I have every right*
> *to ask questions and to get answers for those questions.*
> *The old Diane would not want to have bothered anyone*

and probably would not have called Regions Emergency. But this new updated model called as soon as I got out of bed today.

Sunday, November 14, 2004
Day 209

A WEEK OR so ago Obid asked me if I would be willing to share my "faith story" at our new celebration service at church today. I did pretty well until I got to the last few pages when I'm talking about everything that was done for me by my "earth angels". I looked up and half of the congregation was crying and that did me in. By the time I finished, I think most all were crying. Many of them were my "earth angels." Here is my story:

"When Obid asked me last week to give my Faith Story today, he also wisely added "make it 10–15 minutes". Butch, my husband, tells me that I need grease fittings in my jaws to keep them in work-ing order. Go figure, huh? So with only 10–15 minutes, I decided to talk about my faith story through my recent breast cancer experience in the hope that my story will be of help to any of you facing troubles of any sort in you life. My story, as you know, has a happy ending. My cancer is gone, no chemo or radiation was needed just some very radical surgery. Not all stories turn out this way as we all know. I'm very blessed and very grateful. God sent many "earth angels" to care for me—but I'm getting ahead of my story… Way back a hundred years ago when I was confirmed, our minister assigned me this Bible verse; Psalm 46:1 "God is our refuge and strength, a very present help in trouble". My fifteen year old brain couldn't get around that one at the time. I was offended to think that he thought I was going to be in trouble a lot in my life. My fifty-six year old brain tells me that he was a very wise man. Age and life experience have taught me that this verse was for me a compliment of the highest form. His belief was that my faith was strong enough to see me through the troubles that I as well as everyone else are destined to face in our life time.

Psalm 46: 1–3 "1. God is our refuge and strength, a very present help in trouble. 2. Therefore we will not fear, though the earth should change, though the mountains shake in the heart of the sea; 3. Though its waters roar and foam, though the mountains tremble with its tumult."

My earth began to shake and change and the mountains tremble when my breast cancer "trouble" began in October of 2003. I went in for my yearly mammogram and was called back two days later as some calcifications were found on my right breast. It was decided that an attitude of let's keep a close eye on this for six months would be in order. I made the appointment for April 19– six months to the day—to have a magnification type of screening done. I put it totally out of my mind for five and a half months. Then as the date was nearing I noticed in the mirror that my right nipple seemed to be about an inch lower than my left and that the right breast appeared somewhat larger. Then I remembered my Mom telling me after her mastectomy, that she had watched her breast grow and change until she couldn't stand it any longer and went to see her doctor. I pretty much froze with the realization of what I was now seeing on my own body.

April 19 found me strangely calm. I had been asking God to give me strength to face whatever was ahead for me. Philippians 4:6-7; "Do not worry about anything, but in everything by prayer and supplication with thanksgiving let your requests be made known to God. And the peace of God which surpasses all understanding, will guard your hearts and your minds in Christ Jesus." The peace of God was with me at this moment but would waver as the roller coaster ride of breast cancer was about to take over my life. After the magnification type of screening was over, it took about ten minutes for the doctor to come in to tell me that I was looking at a 20% chance of what they saw being malignant. I told him about my mother. He then explained that on a scale from 1 to 5, 1 being benign and 5 being malignant, I was about a 3. I'm no math whiz but I think my odds just changed rather quickly. The biopsy was scheduled for April 22. The days leading up to that were filled with fear, tears, love, prayers and a whole lot of work. I pressure washed the deck as well as all of the deck furniture. I washed windows, moved plants from one garden to another, cleaned my house from top to bottom - anything to keep from thinking.

As hard as I tried to make it all go away and as hard as I tried to go back in time before this all started, it was not possible. I knew where I was and where I wanted to be and the only way to get there was to travel straight through what ever lie ahead. To get from there to here, I had to take the journey. April 22 dawned along the next step - the biopsy. As I walked into the hospital that morning, I knew that this was just the beginning of many hospital and doctor visits. I had a premonition that malignancy would be found. Where now was the peace of God I had prayed for? The actual biopsy took quite a long time as I had two areas that needed to be looked at. As I lay on my stomach in a rather awkward position on a very strange table, I recited over and over in my head every Bible verse, prayer, and hymn that I could bring to mind. Remembering the peace that the 23rd Psalm brought to Sharon Ewald,(a member of our congregation who died a few years ago of cancer) I said it over and over and over until the procedure ended. Now the waiting for results began. I was told it took 48 hours to run the necessary tests on the tissue taken. However, since it was Thursday, it would probably be Monday before I would have the results. The weekend brought lots of phone calls and emails from family and friends. They couldn't take the threat of cancer away but they could give me their love and support so I didn't feel so all alone. Butch, Krisi and Jeff provided that same love and support as well.

The waiting continued… the days slowly passed by. I worried, I fretted, I cried, I prayed and my family suffered along with me every step of the way. No news on Monday. The waiting continued… My journal entry on Tuesday reads: and I quote:

> "The Psalmist wrote, "Turn to me and be gracious to me, for I am lonely and afflicted. Relieve the troubles of my heart, and bring me out of my distress." Psalm 25:16-17. This is the <u>Daily Guideposts</u> reading for today. Even though I still have not heard my results, I've decided that enough is enough. I'm choosing to live my life as the true gift it is and not obsess and continue to worry over whatever it is in my breast. I will know when I'm supposed to know and will handle it at that time. I've wasted too many days being overly concerned regarding this issue. It's hurting me and my family way too much and it is time to move on. So here we are. Tuesday morning and my life must go on. I encouraged both Butch & Krisi to go to work. They listened to me and decided to do just that. I have more energy than I've had for the last week. The sun is shining and I want to get out in my gardens. The weeds are already getting ahead of me. I know that whatever the results bring, we will be able to handle the days ahead. I have the love and support of family and friends and with God beside me I will make it. Perhaps this is my lesson—perhaps this is where I needed to arrive on my journey through this trial." End quote.

Finally Wednesday morning my gynecologist called with the results. A few days later than I was told I would have the results wouldn't you say? Breast cancer definitely confirmed. She had taken

the liberty of setting up an appointment for me with a breast cancer specialist and surgeon that very afternoon. Can you say mastectomy? It is a very harsh word when you are talking about your own
body. We left the surgeon's office with pamphlets, appointments, and
books. I now knew what I was facing and that I had some huge decisions to make with the help of God and my family. Psalm 46:1 "God
is my refuge and strength, a very present help in trouble." Surgery
was scheduled for May 13. Anger swelled within me. Why me God?
Why now? I don't have time to deal with this at this point in my life.
I don't want my life disrupted with doctor appointments and all that
goes along with it. The anger became so great that I even called my
plastic surgeon a donkey (well that's not the word I used but you get
the point) on our first meeting. I was extremely rude. His office was
the last place in the world that I wanted to be. I hate plastic flowers
let alone plastic body parts.

In spite of my attitude, the "earth angels" continued to minister
to me. I could see and feel God's hand everywhere. I would be in the
midst of making decisions regarding the upcoming surgery... Do I
have them take only the breast with cancer or do I have both breasts
taken? Do I need or want reconstruction? Can I have reconstruction started the same day? The telephone would ring and a nurse or
doctor or a breast cancer survivor would be on the other end ready
to listen and or share their experiences and cry with me. I'm serving
on the Board of United Theological Seminary. The chairman of the
committee I've been assigned to called and shared her breast cancer
story with me. She told me that my job for the next several months
was survival. Now was that the hand of God or what? I had no idea
she was a survivor before that point. Bryan Olson, our youth pastor, emailed me and asked for my permission to have my name and
circumstances lifted in prayer throughout the seminary community.
My response was, "Yes, of course. How many women in my situation
have an entire seminary praying for them? It certainly won't hurt."
Angels in the form of Obid & Margo came to visit as well as sisters-

in-law and sisters in spirit and friends and neighbors. Butch and Krisi were ever present angels that held me, cried with me and loved me.

Decisions were made. Surgery happened and the healing of body, soul and mind began. And still the angels came. Butch and I joked about the delivery trucks backing in and out of our driveway on the Saturday I came home from the hospital. Flowers filled my living room. I told Butch that it smelled like a funeral home in our house. He assured me that it was better than a funeral home as I was alive and could enjoy the fragrance and beauty of the bouquets and arrangements! Others sent cards and still others brought food. Others made phone calls and sent emails and still others supported Butch and Krisi in ways I don't even know. Angels ministered to me through the music of Don Moen and his God Will Make a Way CD and the poetry of Carolyn Salter and the Breast Cancer Support Group in Hastings. Others came and vacuumed, ironed, dusted and scrubbed. Some sent bracelets. Others drove me to my many appointments. Others sent gifts of books, chocolate, wine and comfy pajamas. The flow of love and strength and healing continued. Prayers were being said for me from coast to coast as well as in Canada and Australia. Prayer does make a difference folks. Prayer and love lifted me and carried me through my journey from there to here. I thank you again my dear "earth angels" for whatever part you played in making that happen for me.

I've learned many lessons throughout this experience;

1. It's God's timetable not mine.
2. Prayer works.
3. I am loved deeply by many especially Butch & Krisi.
4. Life is good. The trees are greener and the sky bluer on this side of cancer.
5. Life is too precious to waste and too short to worry over the little things.
6. Choose gratitude –it's a better attitude.

I'd like to close with two poems from Carolyn Salter. Carolyn is a friend of mine that lives in Walcha, NSW, Australia. She lost her brother and mother to cancer and a son to a crop dusting accident. She is highly involved in Australian Relay for Life cancer research fundraising. These two poems are from her book entitled <u>Hurdles are for jumping</u> that was written especially for the Relay for Life event in her community.

Life Was So Easy

By Carolyn Salter

Life was oh so easy
How could I then know
That this was a path
Down which I would have to go?
No options for me
Journeying with dread
Heavy, awful, arduous,
The path that I must tread.

How could I then know
How much that I would learn?
And the friends that I would make
Who would with each other turn
The negatives to positives
Finding easier ways
Trusting in each other
To lighten heavy, difficult days.

How could I then know
How my perspective would change?
And see my life go right way up
Drastically rearrange.
Life's noticeably different now

Little things become so dear
Troubles once insurmountable
Much Simpler now, and clear.

Could I even thank
This strange experience I had?
Will you think me crazy
When I say that I am glad
That this cancer came along
To wake up my whole world?

And now I'm navigating life
With every sail unfurled.

Thank You

By Carolyn Salter

Thank you for this wonderful day
Thank you for science
The doctors and nurses
Committed to cure.

Thank you
For simple sunshine
For birds
Crashing waves
White laced on a turquoise sea
For sunsets
Sunrises
And flowers.

Thank you
For the universe
I marvel at its enormity
And tiny ants
Wondering if they see me as huge
In their world.

Thank you for family
And friends

More precious than any jewels
Thank you
For another opportunity
But most of all
Thank you
For life.
Amen

It felt good to share this story today with people that I've know all of my life. Perhaps it is part of the healing process for me and I did get to thank again so many of my "earth angels" publicly in that way. I had hoped not to cry, but I guess that wasn't possible with so many close friends and family in the congregation. My hope was to help others that are in the midst of turmoil and strife. I received a lot of hugs and positive feedback as I left the church. I guess we really never know how our words affect others.

Tuesday, November 16, 2004
Day 211

I HAD MY three week after surgery check up today with the plastic surgeon. He said that everything looks really good. He removed a couple of stitches that were sticking out. The scars are healing nicely but he suggested that I use a silicon product to help reduce the redness of the scars and keep them soft. Also in an effort to keep things soft, he demonstrated for me some exercises to use with my new breasts on a twice daily basis. It's just pushing the implants up and holding for thirty seconds, pushing them toward the center and holding, and pushing them outward and holding again for the thirty seconds. That way my body will hopefully not make a stiff or hard cavity around the implants and they will remain more pliable in nature. He said he would see me in one month and at that time we would talk about nipple reconstruction.

> *I'm seriously thinking about not going any further with the reconstruction stuff. I'm very happy where things are now. I do not wear a bra of any sort and I'm very comfortable. If I have nipples created, I'd only have to wear a bra to cover them up. So why do it? I am so happy to be on this side of things at this point. I really don't*

want any more surgery for a while. I'll listen to what he has to say because information is good but I'm leaning at this time towards no nipples. We'll see.

I could not find the product that the plastic surgeon suggested but I did find something called "Scar Therapy" that works the same way as he described. The medication is on an adhesive strip that you wear over the scar area for 24 hours. Then you change the strip and continue on for approximately eight weeks at which time you will see a softening of the scar area and a fading of the redness. *It's worth a try. A little expensive but what isn't that works?*

Thursday, December 9, 2004
Day 233

I'M CONCERNED THAT my implants may be moving under my arms more as I seem to be able to feel them more with my arms at my sides. I've been shopping for a bra with a wide band that would help hold in my sides and feel better to my under arms.

Shopping has not been easy. First of all it is difficult to find a 38 A or B cup that has a wide band on the sides. My fat hangs over the narrow little bands and does not look or feel very great. Size 40 does not come in an A cup. To add to the difficulty, not all brands have the same size cups. They all need to be tried on for proper fit. Yesterday afternoon I tried on every style bra in Herbergers but found none that fit. Either the A cup was too small or the B cup was just a little too big. It seemed to bunch up in the middle with a wrinkle and not lie flat.

I tried again this afternoon at Marshall Field's in Minneapolis. I ended up with a Champion brand bra made for more casual wear. The B cup was again a little too roomy. Maybe if I wash it in hot water and dry it in the dryer it will fit better.

Krisi and I were shopping again and she observed, "Whoever thought Mom that you would be looking for an A cup!" Such a problem to have! I guess I'll just go braless. I'll have to ask the plastic surgeon about this next week at our appointment.

Tuesday, December 14, 2004
Day 238

I HAVE ANOTHER check up with the plastic surgeon this morning. Everything is going fine. My left breast is somewhat softer than the right. The scar and everything on the right looks and feels more constricted for some reason. The doctor thought perhaps the extra surgery replacing the damaged tissue expander may be the cause. He didn't seem too concerned about it. He said that everything looked great and that he would see me again in two months and then after that once a year to fulfill the requirements of the silicone implant study. Nipple reconstruction and the tattooing will be discussed at that next appointment.

I asked about wearing a bra and whether or not he thought that would be necessary. My concern was that the implants might start floating around and wind up up on my shoulder or under my arms. He just grinned and assured me that that would not happen. I explained how one of my friend's implants had moved higher on her chest. He felt that that had happened because of a mistake made when the implant was first put in to the body. The muscle had not been expanded enough before the implant surgery and therefore allowed the implant to move. In answer to my question about the bra, he told me that at first it is not advisable. The implant needs to settle in and allow gravity to do it's work. The implant sags and pulls down to make the breast appear more natural and not so round. Wearing a bra at first, can cause the implant to become more shaped like the bra with less of a natural look.

In spite of what he says, I still feel a little more comfortable wearing a bra as it holds in the fat more under my arms. That underarm stuff has been a problem for me all along. I just don't like the feel of my arms rubbing against that part of my body. It feels like I have too much in the way. I had the same problem with my natural breasts and wearing a bra made me feel better. I will however, follow his advice and not start wearing a bra just yet. His nurse didn't think that at this point it would make too much difference. She encouraged me to do whatever I was most comfortable with. I've trusted his advice so far and so far he has been right.

Friday, December 17, 2004
Day 241

I WAS BUSY on my computer today when the dog started making a fuss barking and growling. Then I heard a knock at the door. Our friend Jim, who was a neighbor and moved to Cloquet, MN a number of years ago, was at the door. He stepped inside and folded me into his arms with a huge hug. We hadn't seen him since my initial surgery. He recently had undergone some heart surgery himself. I stepped back from his hug and pulled my sweatshirt tight around my body and made some remark about the "new" me. His reply was instant, "You haven't changed a bit. You are still the Diane that we know and love. You are you not a pair of breasts. You are still you and always will be. The rest of that does not matter at all and don't ever forget it!"

Wow! Quite an affirmation from a man's man! He certainly made my day. Many of Butch's male friends, the ones I do not know real well, are now beginning to talk to me about my surgery and all that followed. I guess it took them the six to seven months to feel comfortable doing so. Our close friends, male and female, had no problem supporting me immediately. I took my daughter's wise advice back at the beginning of this when I was sure no one would look me in the face anymore but would instead be looking at my breasts. She counseled me to come up with some kind of a wise remark that would cause some laughter and break the ice. It worked. It showed people that I was comfortable with my body and that they should be too and that it was okay to talk and ask questions. Hopefully I've been able to help people understand breast cancer and the reconstruction process through my willingness to share. It is also very healing for me to do.

Wednesday, February, 2, 2005
Day 289

OUR BREAST CANCER Support Group decided to start meeting on the first Wednesday of each month in the morning at a local coffee house in addition to our regular meeting on the third Wednesday evening of each month. We decided this for a few reasons. First of all we enjoy one another's company. Secondly it seems like a long time between meetings if you are feeling the need for help, support and camaraderie. Thirdly some women do not like to drive after dark and find the morning time much easier for them to be a part of the group. Today was the first of these new coffee meetings and we had a pretty good turnout. Some of the women came and went as their schedules allowed. We laughed, talked, listened and shared for about two hours. Anne, the youngest member of our group, brought a framed postcard that she has hanging in her bedroom. The picture is of a nude woman who has had a mastectomy of her right breast. She is standing tall in the wilderness with her arms outstretched to the sky and a confident smile on her face as she gazes upward. Her body is strong and healthy as she reaches toward heaven. Where her breast had been is a beautiful tattoo of a vine covering the scar. She is called the "Warrior". Anne explained how the picture has been instrumental in giving her hope and courage as she continues her journey with breast cancer. She finds comfort in the strength that the woman portrays and uses her as a role model to emulate.

> *Each of the women in this group has their own story of their battle. They are all strong, loving, caring women with much to give and much to teach to those around them. I'm so glad that Mickey, one of the group leaders, invited me to join.*

Tuesday, February 15, 2005
Day 302

I MET WITH the plastic surgeon this morning for my regular checkup and a consultation regarding nipple reconstruction and tattooing. My left breast is slightly lower than my right. We talked about how he could do a little nipping and tucking to bring it up and make them more even. After giving it a little thought and realizing it would mean more surgery even though only minor, I declined. I never was perfectly symmetrical before so why should I want to be now? I'm happy and braless and most comfortable.

The nipple reconstruction would also be just a minor surgery. He would use local anesthesia and something else to relax me and hopefully put me out. The incision would be made along the existing scar where he would make to flaps of skin that could be brought up and sewn together to make the nipple. The size of the incisions would depend upon how up right I would want the nipples to be. The tattooing would happen two to three weeks later to add the color around the nipple area creating the areola. As usual, his explanations were very thorough and he was most patient to answer all of my questions. My decision was not to have the nipple reconstruction done. If I were younger, I perhaps would have given this option more thought. However, Butch assures me that he is happy just having me here and healthy. I'm happy being here and healthy so for the time being the answer is no. If I change my mind, this surgery can be done at any time in the future.

I said my good byes for now as I do not need to return again until the one year anniversary of my initial surgery. Each year for five years I will need to make that visit to fulfill the requirements of the silicone study that I needed to be a part of in order to have the implants. They assured me that I should call at any time if I have questions or concerns in the mean time. *Wow! I can't believe I'm **here!** Is the nightmare really over for now? Is everything really done? Will I be okay without these visits? Thank you God. **Let's get on with life!***

> *This journey that started last April has now occupied ten months of my life. Standing "here" and looking back to "there", the time seems to have flown. I couldn't have said that in April as looking ahead for ten months seemed like an eternity. It is funny how time works in that way. It has been a long arduous life changing journey and yet it only took ten months! The lessons I have learned and the alterations to my body, mind and soul have been transformational and yet it only took ten months. I am comfortable with my new body. I can look at my new breasts with their fading red, purple and white scars crossing each horizontally and see beauty and fresh new life. I'm proud of them and the courage they stand for. I see myself as a warrior and I have the scars to prove it and yet it only took ten months. I'm still too chicken to have my ears pierced but I made the decision to have both of my breasts removed in order to save my life. Will the cancer reappear? No one has the privilege of knowing that answer this side of heaven. I do know that if it does reappear I have the strength, love and support, and fortitude to face the battle and that only took ten months to prove to myself as well. I've made*

the journey from "there" to "here". I'm different than I was ten months ago. I'm thankful for the journey and for those yet to come. Without this journey would there have been anymore?

The Survivor

By Carolyn Salter from
<u>Hurdles are for jumping</u>

I have beaten it
It is gone
No more cancer for me
I'm a lucky one
Mine has been cured
Did I do something differently
From those who did not survive?
Is life really
A huge lottery
With God plucking us
Like weeds
To go or to stay?
If so
Am I a flower or a weed?
Which is which?
Does it matter?
I am alive
I am well
I will live this life
Fully
With thanks.

But at the end
I will have
More questions

Many more questions.

Cured Of Cancer

By Carolyn Salter

Cured of cancer!
Another go at life
When it could have been
So different.
Another chance to live my best
And the best is yet to come.
For I have looked at death
And found it
Not frightening
Surprisingly, not frightening.
Merely sadness at the thought
Of leaving those I love
Of leaving all that is familiar.
But death itself.
No
Perhaps merely the method of death
I wish I could choose.
But slipping the confines of a used-up body
To fly free
To return to the Source
That almost entrances me

Exhilarating thought.

I Wonder

By Carolyn Salter

I wonder if I did choose this
If I thought I would gain
Grow
With this experience
Learn, develop
Evolve into a higher soul
Soar.
Closer to perfection.
Then
When I could not know of human pain
Of the wrench
Desolation
Contemplating the possibility
Of leaving this earth.
Of leaving the love of human family
Such love.

Did I choose this then?
When I was still with God
And knew I would return.
And did He say
This will be hard
But I will be with you?

And did I forget all
When I came here
Struggling to make sense of it
Remembering only vaguely
Vaguely a purpose
A conviction that there was
More to do
More ways to grow.
But how, what was it?
And have I found it now?
Have I followed my path?
Am I fulfilling my dreams
Of long ago
Before I was?
And, if so
Is He pleased?

Email from a friend on 2/19/05 (author unknown):

Dear God,

I want to thank You for what you have already done.

I am not going to wait until I see results or receive rewards, I am thanking you right now.

I am not going to wait until I feel better or things look better, I am thanking you right now.

I am not going to wait until people say they are sorry or until they stop talking about me, I am thanking you right now.

I am not going to wait until the pain in my body disappears; I am thanking you right now.

I am not going to wait until my financial situation improves, I am thanking you right now.

I am not going to wait until the children are asleep and the house is quiet, I am thanking you right now.

I am not going to wait until I get promoted at work or until I get the job, I am going to thank you right now.

I am not going to wait until I understand every experience in my life that has caused me pain or grief, I am going to thank you right now.

I am not going to wait until the journey gets easier or the challenges are removed, I am thanking you right now.

I am thanking You because I am alive.

I am thanking You because I made it through the day's difficulties.

I am thanking You because I have walked around the obstacles.

I am thanking You because I have the ability and the opportunity to do more and do better.

I am thanking You because FATHER, YOU haven't given up on me.

Amen

This prayer feels once again like it was written just for me. In spite of my weaknesses and impatience, God's grace has seen me through this breast cancer journey. I am eternally grateful and I will strive "to do more and do better"! Praise be to God!

Part III

Resources for More Help

Along my journey <u>From There to Here,</u> I have found and have been given many resources that were of tremendous help to me. I've included them here so you will not have to search too far for them yourself. They are divided into two sections: Medical Information and Inspiration and Support. My hope is that they will be of assistance to you in your journey or in your ministry of helping others.

Medical Information

Books:

<u>Ask the Doctor:</u> **Breast Cancer,** by Vincent Friedewald, M.D., Andrews and McMeel, 4520 Main Street, Kansas City, Missouri, 64111, 1997.

Pamphlets:

<u>Breast Cancer Dictionary,</u> American Cancer Society, No.4675-CC <u>www.cancer.org</u>

<u>Breast Reconstruction Following Breast Removal</u>, American Society of Plastic Surgeons, 444 East Algonquin Road, Arlington Heights, Illinois 60005, <u>www.plasticsurgery.org</u>.

<u>Breast Surgery: From Biopsy to Reconstruction</u>, Krames Communications

<u>Exercises After Breast Surgery</u>, Reach for Recovery, American Cancer Society, 98-20M-No.4668-CC, 1998.

<u>Mastectomy: A Patient Guide</u>, American Cancer Society, 1997, 97-75M-No. 4600-CC, <u>www.cancer.org</u>

Reach to Recovery Breast Prosthesis Shopping List, American Cancer Society, Midwest Division, Inc., MW531.5, 2001. www.cancer. org

Taking Time: Support for People With Cancer and the People Who Care About Them, National Cancer Institute, NIH Publication No. 97-20599, 1997.

Inspiration and Support

Books:

Beneath His Wings, Abiding in God's Comfort and Love, Paintings by Carolyn Shores Wright, Harvest House Publishers, Eugene, Oregon 97402

Chicken Soup for the Surviving Soul : 101 Healing Stories About Those Who Have Survived Cancer, compiled by Jack Canfield… et al. Health Communications, Inc., Deerfield Beach, FL, www. hci-online.com or www.chickensoup.com, 1996.

Daily Guideposts 2004, Guideposts Books & Media Division, Caramel, New York 10512, www.guideposts.com

Daily Guideposts 2005, Guideposts Books & Media Division, Caramel, New York 10512, www.guideposts.com

Hurdles are for jumping, perceptions of cancer, Carolyn Salter, "Wanderriby", Walcha, NSW 2354, email: dcsalter@northnet. com.au

Illuminata: Thoughts Prayers, Rites of Passage, Marianne Williamson, Random House, NY, 1994.

Once upon a shooting star, by Carolyn Salter, Seaview Press, P.O. Box 234, Henley Beach, South Australia 5022, www.seaview-press.com.au, 2002.

Music CDs:

Don Moen: God Will Make a Way, www.integritymusic.com

Don Moen: I Will Sing, www.integritymusic.com

Chapter 1

My Healing Chair

I, not events, have the power to make me happy
or unhappy today. I can choose which it shall be.
Yesterday is dead, tomorrow hasn't arrived yet. I have
just one day, today, and I'm going to be happy in it.

—Groucho Marx

CORIN ROSCOE, AN antique storeowner, received a gift of a chair from a strange timeworn woman who maintains Jesus built it. She told him it was time he take his turn to care for chair and left. A young asthma patient accidently sat in the chair and two days later was completely healed. The novel, *The Chair* written in 2011 by James Rubart, is a story of romance, danger, mystery, betrayal and most of all healing and restoration. "This tale of unimaginable sacrifice and unconditional love will tug at your heart long after you've completed the last page." Book Review by Bill Myers

My healing chair is full of incredible sacrifice and a love with no conditions or limitations. The story is not mysterious or danger filled. It does however have a lot of healing and restoration involved. It certainly is not the chair from Rubart's novel but it does have a powerful story. It was made by La-Z-Boy in the early 1970's not the Master Carpenter from Bethlehem. Let me share its story with you.

Breast cancer had no history in our family and until it found my mother in 1971. At that time in polite society you under no circumstances talked about such things as this women's disease let alone even said the word b- r- e- a- s- t in mixed company. That hush hush attitude of society no longer exists today. Mom's diagnosis and resulting mastectomy of her left breast was pretty shocking, gruesome and horrific and more so because she was alone in the struggle. Alone only in that at that time you did not share with those around you such personal information. Perhaps she shared with Dad but I know she did not share any of it with me until much later in her life and mine. All of her lymph nodes, breast tissue and some of the muscle were removed from the effected area leaving her with a large concave hollow where her breast had been and diminished ability to use her left arm. Chemotherapy was not an option in the 70's so her follow-up treatment choices were a huge dose of radiation or nothing at all. Fear of the cancer returning and/or metastasizing to the right breast, helped to make the decision to undergo the radiation. This would mean a fifty-mile round trip into St. Paul daily—five days a week for as long as she could endure. Both of my parents were in their late forties and both were employed. The diagnosis of course meant that Mom's treatment would require her to quit her job.

With one salary gone, Dad simply had to keep working to keep up with the household bills and now the medical bills. My husband and I were newlyweds. I was in my first year of teaching and my husband and his family owned and operated a gravel business and also had the responsibility of the snowplowing for Denmark Township where we lived. With winter coming and the gravel business being seasonal; he offered to drive my Mom to her daily treatments so my Dad could continue working without interruption. As a thank you gift for his driving services, of which he would accept no pay, my parents gave Butch a beautiful La-Z-Boy for our new home the following Christmas. Through a bit of serendipity this is the chair that would become my own healing chair years later.

Mom continued the radiation until her skin in the area was black and raw. Medical science regarding breast cancer and cancer in general has come such a long way since the early 70's. Thankfully the grueling radiation treatments gave her twenty-five more years of a good and fairly healthy life. In 1996, she began to experience some heart issues. A massive heart attack surprisingly took her life, as she was about to undergo a testing procedure in preparation for open-heart surgery. Shortly after Mom's death, I received a phone call from her internist. The doctor explained to me that Mom's heart had been injured during the long ago radiation treatments. Under Mom's direction, no one in the family was to be told about this heart condition. "There is an art and a science to being a doctor", she explained. "With your Mom I was functioning under the art side of things. Now that she is gone, I wanted you to know the truth of the matter." Ironically the radiation was responsible for both her living and her dying.

During the next thirty-three years the chair rocked our baby, cradled my dying father on his last visit to our home, supported many bottoms through countless football and hockey games on TV and embraced numerous bodies taking that much longed for nap. It propped up our daughter through chicken pox, the flu and countless colds. It saw innumerable parties, celebrations and holidays and held up pretty well under the teenage attack. It supported me through hours of reading and studying as I worked on my advanced degree. It underwent multiple scrubbings and cleanings and even experienced several trips to be reupholstered. It moved from the living room to the family room and back to the living room. The chair continues to this day to be one of the most loved and comfortable pieces of furniture in our home. My husband has once again claimed it as his own.

2004 brought breast cancer into my life once again. This time I was not one of the caregivers. The disease had invaded my body and I was faced with the challenge of the breast cancer journey. The chair held me as the fear of the unknown washed over me along with the tears. In times of prayer and decision-making I sought the comfort and warmth of the chair. The night before my surgery the chair supported me as I sat with my Pastor and his wife. Secondly a group of my close teaching friends and I spent the evening giving and receiving strength from one another as only genuine friends can do. As the evening was getting later and later, I told my friends that they didn't have to stay any longer. I'd be just fine alone and that Butch would be along shortly. Come to find out, he was waiting just up the road at his shop until he saw a group of cars go by signaling that my friends were gone and he should come home. They on the other hand were waiting for him to come before they felt comfortable leaving me by myself.

My bilateral mastectomy took place on May 13. I was the first surgery on the schedule that morning. By May 15, I was more than ready to head home to my healing chair. I was a bit concerned regarding the drain tubes and the pain pack both extra things that made getting around a little awkward. The pain pack was appealing as it fed pain medication through a tiny tube directly into my incisions. However, it also came with a black bag and a shoulder strap. So good-bye pain pack. The nurses carefully trained Butch in taking care of my four drain tubes. With pages of instructions and appointments along with a package of bandages, rubber gloves, ace wraps, pain pills and even a product to dry wash my hair, we headed home. What a beautiful day! I don't remember the weather outside—but inside the car it was warm and sunny. I had the surgery behind me and was going home to heal and be restored.

My sister-in-law and her husband had carried the healing chair up from the family room into the living room and placed it in front of our large bay window overlooking the driveway. What a perfect spot for me to watch the goings and comings and to heal. I had Butch cover the chair with a quilt that my one grandmother had pieced and my other Grandmother had finished with the batting, backing and quilting. I felt in a sense wrapped in both of their love.

I used bed pillows to prop up my arms and to keep handy in case I needed something to hug while I coughed or sneezed. Butch installed a new wall mount TV in what was becoming my healing corner. He plugged a telephone in within my reach and moved my CD player so that I could operate it with the remote control. My pills and water were close at hand and the bathroom just a very short walk down the hall. Talk about comfort and love! I was hurting but it felt so wonderful to be home and on the healing side of things. Spoiled and so blessed.

From my vantage point of the chair, Nurse Butch and I watched the delivery trucks coming and going all afternoon. By evening my living room was filled with beautiful arrangements and living plants. We laughed together about how it smelled like a funeral home only much much better. "You are alive and here to enjoy all these gifts. I think that is truly better," was his comment. And appreciate I did. I spent the next few days in my chair listening to Don Moen's CD, God Will Make a Way, sleeping and resting, praying for a complete recovery, and taking my meds to keep the pain at bay. The chair was my comfort haven. The gift given to Butch for driving Mom to her radiation treatments for breast cancer was now bringing me security and reassurance as I dealt with the same disease. I call that serendipity.

For about three weeks, I lived my life in the healing chair only getting out to visit the bathroom and to keep my doctor appointments which were many. I ate my meals, slept for the evening, napped on and off all day, and directed housekeeping tasks from my chair. Following teaching a full day of eighth grade English, my daughter would stop by to give my husband a break. She'd take over doing the day to day tasks of keeping a household running smoothly. It was awkward watching her doing for me. It was my job after all to take care of the family. I'm the mother. She was living in Stillwater, which is about twenty-five minutes from our home, so often her husband would join us after work for dinner. My parents were both deceased but fortunately I had other family members that came to help out.

A group of friends from church spent a day vacuuming, dusting, ironing, scrubbing the bathrooms, washing clothes as well as cleaning my floors. A lovely bouquet of flowers and a delicious lunch was all a part of the special treatment. I sat in my chair and cried out of thankfulness and love and with a touch of discomfort. Being the one who always did for others, I found it difficult to be on the receiving end of that kind of care. They taught me that being a gracious receiver is important as it allows them to do something for me taking away their helpless feeling in the face of my breast cancer.

When friends stopped in to visit, they would find me in my healing chair. Many brought in the gift of a meal. Butch made a rule that if you brought a meal you had to stay and enjoy it with us. That rule wisely served two purposes; one it brought me out of my chair and to the table, and secondly it allowed me to experience appearing before my friends and family with my new flatter shape for the first time in the comfort of our home now rather than weeks or months later in public. I discovered the best way to handle the emotions of that coming out was with humor. I would make the first remark saying something like, "Well what do you think of the new me?" while sticking out my now flat chest. That allowed my visitors a chance to take a look rather than try to sneak a peek. Of course they were all curious as for most of my life I was rather well endowed to say the least. Once the ice was broken, we could all laugh and move on.

As the days went by and my strength returned, I'd start out the night sleeping in our bed upstairs. Around 2:30 a.m. I'd move downstairs to the chair where I still would find the most comfort and peace. Propping my arms with the pillows was much easier when half sitting up and the pain from the expanders doing their job of expanding my chest muscles was not as uncomfortable in this position. A large security light outside the window allowed me to enjoy the view of our driveway in the wee hours of the morning when sleep would not come. Under the security light, in my healing chair given years ago by my parents, wrapped in my grandmother's quilt, hearing my husband's snoring in our balcony bedroom just above me, I felt safe.

I felt loved and cared for and I felt assured and confident that my life would not be stopped short at this time by breast cancer. Healing was happening and life was returning to normal. Perhaps I should call it a "new normal" as many alterations to my body, mind and spirit had taken place. Combining all of these influences conveyed a noticeable sense of peace. This peace transcends our earthly trials and pains and brings about the calm and harmony crucial to healing, crucial to saving my life and enabling me to grow.

Breast cancer truly is one of those experiences that can change your life. I don't recommend it as a sought after way to bring about personal growth but I can tell you that is what it did for me. Facing a life-threatening challenge of any sort tends to give you a new perspective on life - a new way to look at things. My healing chair allowed me to not only heal my body but my mind and soul as well. It gave me the opportunity to contemplate some of the big questions and the time to deliberate over the answers. I like myself better today after breast cancer.

BC (before cancer) it was all about my timetable and all the things I needed to do, places I needed to go and things I needed to see. I felt that I really did not have the time to mess with this diagnosis. AC (after cancer), I've come to the realization that it is not my agenda or program that is the most important. I wanted the whole journey to be over with yesterday at the earliest as I was too busy to take time for this healing nonsense. There is a lot to be said for this healing nonsense and not taking the time to do it right can and will be more detrimental to your physical, emotional and psychological health.

BC I believed in prayer but for someone else not necessarily me. AC I know what answered prayer feels like. I've experienced the sense of peace and love that prayer, either your own or someone else's for you, can bring. I've learned how to pray and to make my prayers a continuous part of my everyday life—not just at bedtime or before a meal.

BC love was there. It was always a part of my life. Like everyone else, I longed for more love. AC I've discovered how to be open to the love that is all around you. Love can come to you in so many different pathways, through different behaviors and approaches, under different circumstances and certainly through differing traditions. All of that love has always been there. My problem was that I was not always able to see it or feel it for what it was. Perhaps I was too busy to open my eyes and realize that love was there for me all long. For example, there are times when my husband can be very harsh and direct. At one point early in my cancer journey, I had commented that my plastic surgeon was a real jackass. My husband very quietly responded to my remark with, "I wonder who the jackass really is in this situation Diane." Wow, did that open my eyes! It was the turning point in my journey where I stopped feeling sorry for myself and began to work in earnest to cooperate with my medical team to be a part of the solution instead of adding to the problem. My husband loved me so much that he dared to say exactly what I needed to hear.

I now realize more deeply AC that life is so precious and so very good. Subsequent to my diagnosis when I was in the stage of asking why me, I was sure that I would never get to be a grandmother. I knew for a fact that some other woman would have the privilege of being called grandma by my yet to be born grandchildren. I'm happy to say that I now have a nearly eight-year-old granddaughter who calls me grandma every day and a three-year-old grandson that calls me gram gram on a regular basis. Yes, life is good. The grass is greener and the sky bluer on this side of cancer for the reason of my new awareness.

BC my life was good and busy and full. We both had successful careers and lots of friends and lots of things. AC it became clear to me that an attitude of gratitude is an important virtue to possess. It never hurts to be grateful for kindnesses received. That gratefulness worked as a perspective changer in that it made me realize that I already had everything I needed. Melody Beattie says it this way; "Gratitude unlocks the fullness of life. It turns what we have into enough, and more. It turns denial into acceptance, chaos to order, and confusion to clarity. It can turn a meal into a feast, a house into a home, a stranger into a friend." Now that is powerful!

BC I played the part of the caregiver. Helping out when and where I could left me feeling pretty good as well. Not that there is anything wrong with that as long as the person receiving your help is respected and their dignity stays in tact. AC I understood the importance of allowing others to provide for my needs giving them the opportunity to also experience that warm glow of helping others. To find yourself in need of help is perfectly okay and very human. It takes real courage to say I'm experiencing weakness right now. Can you help me?

BC I struggled with being honest regarding my own feelings and needs. Going into the cancer journey, I made up my mind that I would have to be my own advocate and ask honestly for what I needed. When it hurts, say so. When you don't like something, be honest and admit it. AC I still struggle with being honest regarding my own feelings and needs. By outwardly agreeing when you know deep inside that you do not agree, you can really put yourself in a difficult corner in the long run. For example after my cancer journey, I became involved in a project that was much larger than I ever wanted to be a part of. I was running out of time, patience and money. Because of my lack of expressing my true feelings in the first place, I felt caught in the situation. The predicament and confusion resulted in hurt feelings and a broken friendship that would have all been avoided if I had expressed my true feelings in the beginning.

BC I believed that I knew what was best for me. I was very independent in most of my decision making. Being a classroom teacher for twenty-six years tends to make you that way. My husband and a few others were my trusted confidants but I knew I could do most things by myself. It was extremely hard for me to place my trust in anyone but me. AC it became clear that I do need to listen to others and take the time to discern if what they are advising me may just have some merit. My plastic surgeon encouraged me during the final three months of the expansion process to try on different clothes, bathing suits and bras to make sure that I was satisfied and happy with my new breast size before the implants were actually put in. Changing size is possible before the implants but not afterward. I waited the three months of course but didn't bother to check for sizing. After my implant surgery, it became apparent to me that I was between sizes. Had I listened, I would have known that BEFORE and wouldn't still be dealing with that issue now. I have silicone liners that are about a quarter of an inch thick to wear inside my bra to fill it out. I find them heavy and hot so most of the time I go braless. That seems to work the best for me. Silicone does not stretch or sag so I'm pretty perky. Only problem being that I have gained quite a bit of weight. I now have basically four boobs—two where they are suppose to be and one under each arm. Try finding a bra that works for that!?!?!?!

As I said earlier, my healing chair is full of incredible sacrifice and unconditional love. My life is different today than it was before my cancer experience. My healing chair and the lessons learned while convalescing there really have saved my life and hopefully can help you save your life as well. The word convalescing means not only recovering and recuperating but also improving, getting better, reclaiming and rescuing. I believe it is all in your perspective my friends and perspective is something that you can change. I truly believe that breast cancer "saved" my life as in making improvements and making my life better through rescue and reclamation. Does my healing chair possess any magical or mystical powers? No, of course not—the power and the strength to make needed changes in my life was always right here within me. With the help of God and a tremendous nudge from breast cancer, I was able to survive my cancer journey and emerge on the other side more whole than I've ever been before.

I'd like to leave you today with a poem written for my healing by Carolyn Salter of Walcha, New South Wales, Australia. Carolyn was diagnosed with the exact same type breast cancer as mine almost one year later to the day. Her poetry served for her healing as well as my own. My first book, **From There to Here; A Breast Cancer Journey**, is where you will find her healing poems published.

Life Was So Easy
By Carolyn Salter

Life was oh so easy
How could I then know
That this was a path
Down which I would have to go?
No options for me
Journeying with dread
Heavy, awful, arduous
The path that I must tread.

How could I then know
How much that I would learn?
And the friends that I would make
Who would with each other turn
The negatives to positives
Finding easier ways
Trusting in each other
To lighten heavy, difficult days.

How could I then know
How my perspective would change"
And see my life go right way up
Drastically rearrange.
Life's noticeably different now
Little things become so dear
Troubles once insurmountable
Much simpler now, and clear.

Could I even thank
This strange experience I had?
Will you think I'm crazy
When I say that I am glad
That this cancer came along
To wake up my whole world?

And now I'm navigating life
With every sail unfurled!

God's Timetable and Ideas— Certainly not Mine!

Stress makes you believe that everything has to happen right now. Faith reassures you that everything will happen in God's timing!

—Spiritual Inspiration

PATIENCE HAS NEVER been one of my virtues. Whenever I come up with an idea, I want it done yesterday. I have endurance, tolerance and even pretty good stamina but the capacity for waiting for something is pretty far down on my list of attributes. Yes, I taught elementary school for twenty-six years and yes most of that time was in first grade with six and seven year olds. But that kind of patience is different. It takes persistence, a lot of unflappability and an extraordinary amount of staying power to help children learn to read and write. That I have. In fact sometimes a little impatience is even necessary to bring about growth in students.

The patience I'm talking about is the kind you need when you are building a new home and you wanted to move in last month. Or when your husband suffers a stroke and you are impatient for his healing so life can return to normal. Or when you are working on a project for your school or church and it feels like it will never go anywhere. It is kind of like trying to move an elephant by just giving him a shove. Or as our good friend Snoopy puts it, "Life is like an ice cream cone, you have to lick it one day at a time." – that takes the patience I'm talking about. My breast cancer journey demanded that type of patience from me. Over and over again I needed to be reminded that the timetable was not mine to choose. A larger power than myself was in control. Certain things take time and no matter how much I worry or fret and scream and holler, or even push and shove, I cannot change that schedule or hurry that agenda. Whenever I tried, I found myself in a bigger mess.

If I remember right, I had been out of the hospital for a couple of weeks and was beginning to feel better and better. My biggest difficulty and cause for discomfort was the drain tube situation. Post-op patients come back from the OR with usually more than one drain tube. I had four, two under each arm. The drains promote healthy wound healing, prevent infection, and reduce pain. Drains remove blood, serum, lymph, and other fluids that accumulate in the wound after surgery. If allowed to build, these fluids put pressure on the site as well as neighboring organs, vessels, and nerves, causing pain. Not draining these fluids delays healing and in addition the fluid buildup serves as a breeding ground for bacteria. The drains are a necessary evil. I asked the nurse to remove the drains before the weekend as my underarms were becoming more and more sore where the tubes exited my body. She reluctantly did as I had asked. Immediate relief spread over me. It felt so good and my hope was that it would speed up the healing.

The fluids continued to build, however, with no drains to take care of the pressure. By late Saturday afternoon I knew I was in trouble. My chest was so tight and so painful that it was hard to breathe. I called the nurse and she told me the clinic would not be open until Monday morning. I should come in then and they would aspirate the fluid at that time. She also suggested that if I couldn't wait until Monday, to visit the hospital ER where they would do the procedure and then I should come in on Monday to see the doctor. I can't begin to tell you how wonderful it felt to have that fluid removed. At the same time as my initial mastectomy surgery, the plastic surgeon inserted tissue expanders under my chest muscles to make room for the silicone implants. Each week I would go in and have saline solution added to the expander through a magnetic port made for that purpose. The expander grew like a balloon filling with water. Small amounts of solution were added each week as my chest began to expand making room for the eventual adding of the implant. The expander was making a pocket to hold the implant in place. This all was not without discomfort.

Back to my story – bright and early on Monday I arrived at the clinic. On the right side where the needle aspiration had taken place, the expander was soft and rather squishy. The needle aspiration had punctured the expander much like sticking a pin in a balloon. I was back to square one on the right side needing to have surgery to remove the damaged expander and insert a new one. Lesson learned the hard way I might add – back to surgery, back to two new drain tubes and back to starting the healing process again. Instead of speeding up the time frame, I had just added a few more weeks. Everything happens in due time – in God's time not mine. It could not be hurried no matter how hard I tried.

"Don't push so hard. Slow down, take your time. Why don't you just relax and rest," were messages that I was hearing over and over again from family and friends alike. Slowing down for me was like taking a speeding train and running it into a brick wall. Picking yourself up from the other side of the wall and moving at a different rate of speed or not moving, can also be detrimental to your health. Along with learning to trust His timetable, I also learned to be open to other surprises, ideas, and opportunities that came my way. Someone once told me that when God closes a door, He opens a window somewhere else and that He did.

One of the first window's that opened came to me in the person of Mickey O'Connor. As a breast cancer survivor herself and co-leader of the Hastings Breast Cancer Support Group, she called me a month or so after my surgery and asked if she could come and visit. Her husband's family farm adjoined the Davies farm at one point in history. The two families have had a long friendship going back a generation or two. Mickey invited me to attend the next support group meeting with her. I didn't really think I needed a support group but Mickey's invitation was so genuine and heartfelt that I couldn't turn her down. The women involved in this group became some of my best friends. When Mickey's cancer returned, I took on her leadership role with another survivor and good friend, Claire Mathews. I'm no longer a co-leader but still have a very strong relationship with the group and continue to distribute the Voices of Hope DVDs as my contribution.

After becoming a part of the Hastings Breast Cancer Support Group, I became acquainted with A Fitting Place owned and operated by Penny Schields. Penny's sister lost her life to breast cancer and as a tribute to her, Penny became a mastectomy fitter and opened this business for breast cancer survivors. She sold mastectomy bras, forms, prosthesis, bathing suits and sleepwear. As a hairdresser, Penny also cut, styled, permed and took care of the beauty needs of her clients even shaving hair before chemo treatments if that was desired. She was so gentle and loving it was hard not to become her friend. She and I came up with the DVD idea for people newly diagnosed but it became too difficult to mesh the two different messages – the one of support in the physical need and the other support in the emotional need. Through Penny I began to learn many lessons on being an advocate for women with breast cancer.

My husband and I have a summer home on an island in the north arm of Rainy Lake in Ontario. I had heard tell of a legend of a horse that also lived in the same rough country. In the summer the horse would find an island to call home for the season with the island inhabitants supplementing his food supply. As winter came on, he may or may not walk across the ice to a new island. The all year round residents adopted the horse and even hauled hay out across the ice for him in the winter. The legend came to life for me when I actually met the horse on an island a few miles from us. A TV station out of the Twin Cities, KSTP-TV featured both our friends and the horse on "5 On the Road with Jason Davis" in 2004. Author and illustrator, Linda Causton, saw the broadcast. She was so moved by the story that she wrote a children's book based on the horses life entitled, *Lester's Rainy Lake Pony* published by DeForest Press in Elk River, Minnesota. Trying to find a copy of the book, I called DeForest Press and Richard DeForest and Shane Groth came into my life. Richard and I visited for a good hour that day if not longer. I did order the book by the way but also found a publisher for my first book as well. "Everyone's story deserves to be told," he rationalized. "Send me a copy of your manuscript and we'll talk," and so *From There to Here; A Breast Cancer Journey* by Diane Davies came into being. It was truly a God-thing.

The LeDuc Historic Mansion and Estate in Hastings, Minnesota hosted an author event featuring local authors. Being a newly published author I was invited to introduce myself and my new book to the community. Sharing the library with me was Marisha Chamberlain novelist, playwright, poet and librettist. She was introducing her new novel *The Rose Variations.* Between visitors to our respective tables, we had opportunities to chat with each other. Marisha asked, "So what's next Diane? What do you plan to do now?" I shared my idea of producing a DVD for women newly diagnosed with breast cancer that would serve as a virtual support group to offer encouragement and hope for the journey ahead. The Hastings Breast Cancer Support Group, of which I was co-leader at the time, was searching for a way to make that outreach happen. Her reply was, "You know what, I think I can help you with that." And so another collaborator dropped into my life resulting in the production of Voices of Hope-DVD Series for the newly diagnosed breast cancer patient and their caregivers. In 2013 this series won the

CPEN (Cancer Patient Education Network) Excellence in Education Award given at their international conference in Seattle, WA.

Marisha became for me a true mentor and a friend, introducing me to not only the non-profit world but also a world of growth and opportunity. My writing skills greatly improved under her tutelage and as I watched and listened I slowly began to grow into the position of Executive Director of Circle in the Field Peer Support for Breast Cancer that the two of us had founded. She was also responsible for coaching me into and through a Bush Fellowship in 2011 where I grew as a leader and an advocate for breast cancer patients. It was through Bush that I made my biggest leap forward and realized that I was on a course that was taking me away from my family and my goal of touching breast cancer patients in a much more personal way than running a non-profit. This brought me face to face with the realization that I had to be true to who and what I am and want I wanted and loved. I also had to be an advocate for me. A huge lesson learned. As a result, I no longer am involved in Circle in the Field but instead have moved into enjoying retirement and spending time with my family.

Would you believe that car shopping for a new vehicle brought another teammate into my life? God does work in mysterious ways. Tim Braun worked for Inver Grove Ford and Lincoln at the time and was the salesman on duty when Butch stopped in to look at an MKT for me to drive. He was a good salesman as we bought two vehicles from him in pretty short order. During one of our visits to the dealership, Tim and I began to chat about my book and the DVDs that were newly produced. I was looking for a way to get the attention of Ford Motor Co. to help with distribution and such. That's when Tim explained that before the economy "crash" he was in the media business but was now selling cars to keep his family afloat. "I'd like to work with you and help you make some connections for marketing the DVD," and we were off and running. With Tim's help we found a firm that helped us with reproduction, packaging and distribution with a newer and more modern look. He was able to connect us to some financial support and was instrumental in coordinating a grand premier for the second DVD in the series aimed at friends and family of the patient at a theatre in Minneapolis. The premier was complete with a silent auction, a few short speeches and popcorn. As you might guess, he is back in the media business and is no longer selling cars.

A few years ago as I was reading The Breast Cancer Wellness Magazine, I came across a contest that the magazine was sponsoring to honor breast cancer survivor's caregivers. The grand prize was a Caribbean Cruise for two. I filled out the application just for the fun of it and nominated my husband as my special caregiver and mailed it in not giving it another thought. I answered the phone one day and heard this cheerful, "Hi! I'm Beverly Vote, owner and editor of The Breast Cancer Wellness Magazine. I'm looking for Butch Davies." I explained that he was not home at the time but that I would be happy to take a message. She responded with, "Well is this Diane? You nominated him in our caregiver sweepstakes and I'm calling to tell him that he is the grand prize winner." My first thought was, "Boy am I in trouble now." I never told him about entering the contest because who ever wins that stuff anyway and even worse he is the most unpleasant passenger on a cruise. It makes him feel trapped and ornery. My response to Bev was, "Oh how exciting! I'll tell him and have him get in touch with you."

As you can well imagine, Butch wanted no part of the trip. "Why did you even apply for such a thing?" I was wondering that myself now. "Why don't you call her back and have her give it someone that would really enjoy it. It should be a trip of a lifetime for someone – just not me," was his reply. I can only imagine Ms. Vote's surprise when I returned her call and turned down the grand prize. It did become the trip of a lifetime for a young single mom breast cancer survivor and her mother who had been her caregiver. For me it became the beginning of a telephone friendship with Bev and at the same time a number of different opportunities through her magazine for my writing. She too believes that everyone has a story that deserves to be told and in addition that these stories are destined to help others manage their own breast cancer journeys. Bev and I have not met in person as of yet but she is currently encouraging me with her wisdom through the writing of this manuscript. Another teacher and collaborator that just happened to fall into my life by authority of the keeper of the stars.

Are these all coincidences? I truly find that hard to believe. These people came into my life at opportune times to help me with my mission of helping others. Even my teaching career was training for my role now supporting women and men through breast cancer. I am grateful for all of their assistance along the way. I look forward to seeing what else or who else is in store for me and how the roles may be reversed with me being the one to offer guidance and help to another.

Power of Prayer

In my deepest, darkest moments, what really got
me through was a prayer. Sometimes my prayer was
'Help me.' Sometimes a prayer was 'Thank you.'
What I've discovered is that intimate connection and
communication with my creator will always get me
through because I know my support, my help, is just
a prayer away.

—Iyanla Vanzant

SO JUST WHAT is prayer? I'm sure that hundreds of thousands of words have been written on the topic but for me prayer is simply talking with my God. Of course underlying that statement is the belief that there is a God, a higher power, or whatever that spiritual being is called that you may recognize in your life. When I say talking with my God that does imply that I must do some listening as well. In my experience that doesn't mean that God and I actually have a two-way conversation that you could listen in on like on a cell phone. Rather it means that I must be willing to be open and on the alert for ways that God may be speaking to me through my experiences and interactions with others. I want to share with you how important this spiritual connection became to me when diagnosed with breast cancer and the difference it made in my journey and my healing.

Many years ago my Mom and Dad taught my brothers and me to say our prayers before eating by saying; "Come Lord Jesus, be our guest, and let these gifts, to us be blest. Amen". And before bedtime saying; "Now I lay me down to sleep, I pray the Lord my soul to keep. If I should die before I wake, I pray the Lord my soul to take. Amen". We also learned the Lord's Prayer in Sunday school and a number of other grace and bedtime prayers when we stayed with friends in their homes. Prayer, however, is more than reciting a few lines of verse. As I grew older and grew in my faith, I began to comprehend and appreciate more fully this time of prayer and the spiritual connection it represents. It wasn't until a young mother in our congregation was diagnosed with a life-threatening cancer that I truly came to grasp and identify with what this talking to God was really all about.

Sharon sat across the sanctuary aisle from me on the left hand side of the church almost every Sunday. Joining her was her perfect well-dressed family; handsome husband John, and a beautiful son and daughter. Sharon herself always looked like she had just stepped from the pages of a trendy magazine. Fair complexion, strawberry blonde hair, blue eyes and just a hint of freckles across her nose matched seamlessly with her slim frame. Her husband was tall and she herself was just an inch or two shorter. I remember one summer Sunday, Sharon wore a lovely flowery cotton sundress in pastels, a wide brimmed straw hat with a blue ribbon to match her eyes and the blue in her dress and white strappy sandals. She could have floated out of a watercolor painting in someone's solarium. She possessed a bit of flair toward the dramatic like perhaps in a former life she had been an actress or a model and yet she looked every bit the country girl, healthy and strong and in love with life.

A week or so after the flowery sundress Sunday, Sharon called my home requesting my help. I was caught a little off guard as our relationship so far had been one of smiles, handshakes and nice to see you on Sunday mornings. She explained that she had been diagnosed with cancer and that she was putting a prayer team into place made up of some of her friends and some of the women from our church. She invited me to be a part of that team if I would be willing to help her out in this way. She was hosting a coffee party later in the week at her home for potential team members where she would explain her needs and plans and answer our questions.

Eight hesitant women were seated in Sharon's dining room in her yet again perfect country home around a fine-looking antique round oak table. Coffee and an assortment of goodies had been served. Sharon stood charmingly at the head of the table much like a teacher about to address her class. Her gratitude for each of us being there radiated from her lovely face.

Sharon explained how she planned for us to participate in her cancer journey with her by being her prayer team and what that included. Members would each take a day of the week to pray with her regarding her illness and her needs. Her desire was that we would pray with her face to face either meeting her somewhere for coffee or coming to her home. Worst-case scenario, we would use the telephone to connect us. The meeting times would change from week to week according to her scheduled treatments and appointments and the needs of her family.

This will be a huge undertaking of time was the first thing to cross my mind. Secondly, what if God doesn't hear or answer my prayers? What if I really don't know how to pray? Sharon was asking us for our honesty and our questions so I gave voice to my thoughts. She told us that she had chosen us because of what she felt was our strong faith. She went on to explain that the ultimate decision as to whether she would live or die from this disease was in God's hands not ours or her own. She wasn't asking us for a miracle—she was asking us for prayers to support her on this cancer journey. "If I live, praise God. If I die, that is God's will and you will have helped pray me into heaven," was her response.

I became a part of Sharon's prayer team and prayer became a part of my everyday life. I didn't have a specific time set aside each day for prayer, except on days that I would visit Sharon. I found that my day became a continual prayer, asking God for this and thanking Him for that. Sharon became a role model teaching me not only how to pray but how to face the challenge of a disease that was in the end going to take her life. As seems to be always the case, I feel that I received more than I gave throughout the experience.

Sharon continued to decline. Hospice care was started and shortly thereafter, she was moved to the hospital where she could be made more comfortable. The phone rang early the morning of my next prayer day. Sharon's husband, John, wanted us to know how to find her room at the hospital and to tell us that he thought she would really appreciate our visit. He explained that she was feeling restless and quite agitated and that perhaps our visit would help her to be more contented and comfortable. Through our weeks of praying together, Sharon shared with us her love of the Psalm 23 and how it always gave her strength and courage. Having her Lord as her Shepherd provided her with everything she truly needed. Resting in her God gave her renewed power and helped her know what to do and how to act. With death near, she needed Him close by guarding and guiding. He cared for her and gave her many blessings. Goodness and kindness would be with her all her days and after death she would be with her God forever. The Psalm had become her personal statement of faith. We prayed Psalm 23 with Sharon that day and saw the calm that came over her. The lines of worry and sadness were replaced by the now famous for us, Sharon smile. Her breathing straightened out and she rested comfortably with her eyes closed. We continued our prayers and she joined in again as we started on the Lord's Prayer. We said our good byes quietly and left Sharon peaceful and comfortable. The power of prayer and the changes it can bring was so very evident. Sharon passed on later that evening. Even in the face of death, she chose to continue living rather than living to die. She persisted in that choice to the very last step when she achieved acceptance and opened herself to death with grace and dignity. I'm so very grateful to her for showing me the way to prayer.

When my own cancer diagnosis came in 2004, I thought back to Sharon and the strength that she relied on throughout her storm. As her body weakened, her faith became deeper and stronger. I believe that it was her conversations with God, her prayers that brought about her peace. I was witness to that peace descending upon her that day as we prayed in the hospital together. Now as I was looking at my own health challenge, I vowed that I would follow Sharon's lead and rely on prayer to find my own peace.

Once again I slipped into the habit of continual throughout the day kind of prayer. God walked with me through the waiting for results, the surgeries, the healing and the finding of the new normal in my life. My prayers literally were conversations. I didn't have to start each prayer with Dear Lord, or Dear Heavenly Father and end with amen. I just talked – those who know me well know how good I am at that! As far as God's half of the conversation, that came loud and clear through the people around me and their love and concern shown for me whether it was family, friends, or medical staff.

I also learned that prayer could be as simple as listening to my favorite CDs. I'd stretch out in my healing chair, close my eyes and let the music envelope me allowing me to comprehend Psalm 46:10, "Be still and know that I am God". These peace filled times brought healing to my body, mind and soul. The difficult part for me was letting go and letting God but my reward for doing so was the tranquility, harmony and reconciliation that would come bringing to me the freedom to heal.

One Sunday morning recently as I was driving to church, my thoughts were on the writing of this chapter. I felt a bit stuck and was sharing my quandary with God. As I settled into the pew and looked ahead on the bulletin, I discovered that the topic of the day's sermon was "Prayer"! Really? A coincidence? I believe it was not happenstance but rather an answer to my own prayer. I was meant to hear JaNae Westrich's sermon.

Excerpts from "I'm Praying for You" by JaNae Westrich:
John 17:1-22

"It has been said that there are only two places in all of Scripture where the actual prayers of Jesus himself are recorded and that we have knowledge of, those are the Lord's Prayer and this one (The High Priestly Prayer). On the whole, we have a lot of affinity for the Lord's Prayer. Thousands of people say it just about every Sunday. The Lord's Prayer is primarily a prayer of Jesus teaching his disciples and us, vicariously how to pray. It is a prayer that is centered around us. In our recitation of the prayer, there is action taken upon our part, we are praying to God for help, and praying for God to do God's part. In this High Priestly prayer, Jesus begins by praying for himself, then launches into a beautiful prayer for his disciples and then ends with a prayer for all of us. It is a prayer in which Jesus is offering his heart to His Father. Through this prayer, we become the recipients of Jesus' intercession on our behalf and the prayer expresses His care, concern and compassion. In this prayer the High Priestly Prayer, we God's people, take a passive role as the recipients as Jesus prays for us, on our behalf. Jesus prays specifically for continued strength and perseverance in this world. This High Priestly Prayer also delivers a great model for us as we pray for others: The Agape Bible Study offers this format and I would like to share it with you: Jesus first prays for himself, He prays affirming the glory of the cross (verses 1-2), He expresses the essence of eternal life (verses 3-4), He rejoices in the shared glory of the Father (verse 5). He then prays for his disciples He prays for their knowledge (verses 6-9), He prays for their perseverance (verses 10-12), He prays for their joy (verse 13), He prays for their protection from evil (verses 14-16), He prays for their sanctification (verses 14-17) and then he prays for future believers and He prays for their oneness in the Father and the Son (verses 20-22).

Have you ever found yourself saying to someone: I'll be praying for you or we will say a prayer for you and then you think to yourself, ok now what? Or how do I do that? Or what should I say in my prayer? Etc. maybe as we think about how to pray for others, this can be used as a model. Use the High Priestly prayer to be your guide for how and what to pray for. First, offer praises and words of thanksgiving to God, then, pray for yourself, just as Jesus did. Bring your requests to God for whatever you are going through, then offer up your own request for someone else before God. Pray for their continued strength, pray for God's protection around them and pray that the person would persevere with courage till the end. Then offer a prayer up for our world.

I don't know about you but sometimes, a situation arises that renders me speechless in my prayers for someone else or lately our world events have been so tragic, so heartbreaking that I do not know where to begin in prayer. Have you ever felt that way? There is a verse in the Bible that I often fall back upon and put my faith and trust in. It is from Romans 8:26 and it says: "Likewise the Spirit helps us in our weakness; for we do not know how to pray as we ought, but that very Spirit intercedes with sighs too deep for words. 27 And God who searches the heart, knows what is the mind of the Spirit, because the Spirit intercedes for the saints according to the will of God." I take comfort and am grateful for this assurance that when I am in doubt, God knows, God sees and God cares. I take comfort knowing that the Holy Spirit also intercedes for me when I am at a loss for words. That the Holy Spirit knows what needs to be said and prays on my behalf, just as Jesus did for his disciples and for us."

Rev. Westrich ended her sermon with an assignment for her listeners and a practice session for the assignment to help us get started. Each participant was given a small rectangle of paper and asked to think of something that he/she needed prayers for this week. On the paper we were to write one word that would explain what we felt we needed; encouragement, healing, or love for example. The paper would be like a string around our finger to aid us in remembering ourselves in prayer. On the backside of the paper, we were asked to write down these three words; strength, protection, and courage. "Prayer for someone can be as simple as saying the person's name and asking God for strength, protection and courage for that person," explained the Pastor. "Just tuck this little slip of paper on your refrigerator or someplace where you are sure to see it daily," JaNae told us. "When you see it, just say a quick prayer for that person." She keeps her slip in the visor of her car and whispers a prayer when stopped at a traffic light. What a simple way to get started on a life of prayer! I encourage you to give it a try.

So I ask again; what is prayer? I found this answer in a blog called... In the Meantime written by The Rev. Dr. David Lose the Marbury E. Anderson Chair in Biblical Preaching at Luther Seminary in St. Paul, MN. "Here's my hunch: I think prayer has more to do with relationship than "outcomes." We pray, that is, because it is a vital way of remaining in relationship, just as we may pour out our hearts to a friend, lover, or family member not in the expectation that they are necessarily going to do something about it but because we need someone to share with. And as we share all these things the relationship grows stronger. I think that makes more sense to me. Prayer is about relationship.

Lately, though, I've been musing about prayer in another way. Perhaps prayer is also a way of attuning ourselves to God and our shared life. That is, among other things prayer is also a practice. It is a practice where we lift up to God our joys and concerns, dreams and fears, hopes and anxieties. And as we do so we are thinking about all these things in light of our relationship with God and our faith. That in turns means that every time we pray we bridge the gap between our "daily life" and our "faith life."

That resonates with me. When I think about building a relationship with anyone, I realize that we do that by spending time with them, sharing thoughts and feelings, hopes and desires. Talking. So of course that is how we would build a relationship with our higher power.

As you begin or work on strengthening your prayer life and your relationship with your God, here are a few truths to help you;

> Do not be afraid to ask for what you truly need remembering the difference between needs and wants. Asking for help is not a sign of weakness but rather a sign of strength in that you know and understand your needs. It can be an indication of maturity on your part.

> Trust in your Maker whatever your religion may be. There is peace and comfort there for you. This spiritual connectedness is part of the healing that makes you whole.

> Honesty regarding feelings and honesty in communication is so very important for reconciliation, understanding and healing of any kind. This is honesty with your God and honesty with your family and friends. Not doing this you can find yourself backed into a corner pretty easily and end up hurting others rather than helping.

> By reaching out to others, Sharon found others reaching back to help her and her family. Dying is something that you have to do alone but preparing to die does not need to be lonely.

By helping others you do yourself the favor of helping yourself. I've never known this to be anything but true. Invariably when I reach out to others I end up receiving and learning more than I ever expected.

Love Comes to you
in Many Ways...

"To love and be loved is to feel the sun from both
sides."

—David Viscott

LOVE IS DIFFICULT to define. Everyone from philosophers and psychologists, musicians and poets to Sufi Masters and the Bible have tried to define just what love is. Even Charlie Brown and the whole Peanuts Gang define love in Charles Schulz's 1965 book; Love is Walking Hand in Hand. Perhaps love is best described through the simple acts and moments of everyday life. In that case the Peanuts Gang has it pretty well nailed.

Love is Walking Hand in Hand
By Charles Schulz

Love is messing up someone's hair
Love is loaning your best comic magazines
Love is having a special song
Love is tickling
Love is a valentine with lace all around the edges
Love is wishing you had nerve enough to go over
and talk with that little girl with the red hair
Love is letting him win even though you
know you could slaughter him
Love is sharing your popcorn
Love is hating to say good-bye
Love is walking hand in hand
Love is a letter on pink stationery
Love is getting someone a glass of water in the middle of the night
Love is passing notes back and forth in school
Love is standing in a doorway just to see her if she comes walking by
Love is making fudge together
Love is wondering what he's doing right now this very moment
Love is buying somebody a present with your own money
Love is not nagging
Love is visiting a sick friend
Love is a phone call
Love is walking in the rain together
Love is eating out with your whole family
Love is being able to spot her clear across the playground
among four hundred other kids
Love is committing yourself in writing
Love is meeting someone by the pencil sharpener
Love is being happy just knowing that she's
happy… but that isn't so easy
Love is a flag

> Love is liking people
> Love is liking ideas
> Love is the whole world.

Let's take a look at love from the Bible's point of view. This scripture is used many times at weddings because it describes love so well.

1 Corinthians 13 New Living Translation (NLT)
Love Is the Greatest

13 If I could speak all the languages of earth and of angels, but didn't love others, I would only be a noisy gong or a clanging cymbal. **2** If I had the gift of prophecy, and if I understood all of God's secret plans and possessed all knowledge, and if I had such faith that I could move mountains, but didn't love others, I would be nothing. **3** If I gave everything I have to the poor and even sacrificed my body, I could boast about it; but if I didn't love others, I would have gained nothing.
4 Love is patient and kind. Love is not jealous or boastful or proud **5** or rude. It does not demand its own way. It is not irritable, and it keeps no record of being wronged. **6** It does not rejoice about injustice but rejoices whenever the truth wins out. **7** Love never gives up, never loses faith, is always hopeful, and endures through every circumstance.
8 Prophecy and speaking in unknown languages and special knowledge will become useless. But love will last forever! **9** Now our knowledge is partial and incomplete, and even the gift of prophecy reveals only part of the whole picture! **10** But when the time of perfection comes, these partial things will become useless.
11 When I was a child, I spoke and thought and reasoned as a child. But when I grew up, I put away childish things. 12 Now we see

things imperfectly, like puzzling reflections in a mirror, but then we will see everything with perfect clarity. All that I know now is partial and incomplete, but then I will know everything completely, just as God now knows me completely.

13 Three things will last forever—faith, hope, and love—and the greatest of these is love.

Love can encompass everything from liking something very much, to passionate attraction and desire, to having sex with somebody, to a term of friendly address, to worship of God, to even a score of zero as well as something eliciting enthusiasm. Books and more books have been written concerning the subject matter - so what more can I add to the mix? Probably not much.

What makes me feel appreciated and cared for? Twelve years ago as I was experiencing my breast cancer journey, I found love coming to me in many ways; cards & letters, phone calls, a bowl of mushroom soup, gifts of flowers, meals and yummy desserts, wine, a quick visit with a warm hug, pinching my toes or squeezing my hand, finding me a cool pillow or a warm blanket. Butch made his love visible through his tears with me, a tender bath, answering even with a few sharp words that brought me back from my own little pity party. Of course that's love!

What about today? Nature always makes me aware of God's presence and love for me. The manatee swimming just under the surface of the water and the little gecko climbing over the rocks, the sunshine and palm trees, the stars and the moon are all a love note from on high.

Butch catching my eye from across the table during dinner, carrying a bag for me through the airport, checking with me to make sure I wanted the top down on our way home this evening in Faye's Thunderbird are all signs of his love for me.

Calling me or emailing during the day to give me last minute instructions for bus pick-up, inviting me for tacos on Tuesday evening, wanting to spend time with me shopping are ways my daughter shares her love. I remember a time when she was just a little girl that she gave me a quarter from her piggy bank for my birthday. I saved the coin for many years in my jewelry box. In 1996 our house was broken into and my jewelry box was stolen along with the quarter. Knowing how much that quarter meant to me, she placed another one into my hand for me to add to the new jewelry box.

Then there's the grandchildren; the on the run hug that nearly knocks you off your feet, the "I want to stay with Grandma!", "Play with me", "Read to me" are all ways they say "I love you Grandma!"

From January 2014 through January 2015 and perhaps just a little beyond, I took part with a number of members of my church and our Pastor in a Bible Challenge. We pledged to read the Bible from cover to cover in one year. Actually we didn't end up reading it from cover to cover but rather in chronological order, which is different. We had daily reading assignments and monthly pages of questions to answer for our own comprehension and clarity. We also met once a month as a group for moral support and to discuss any topics we were having difficulty with. It truly was an excellent experience that I would recommend to anyone so inclined. An outstanding leader helps pull it all together. At our final meeting of the challenge we summarized the Bible in one word. That word was and is LOVE. If I had to choose a second word it would be relationship. Love and relationship seem to be inseparable to me.

The author's of the Bible and Charles Schulz are certainly in agreement in defining love. I would just add that the receiver must be tuned in in an effort to feel the effects of that love. Without being open and accepting a person could go through life and never realize all of the love that is out there for them. My experiences throughout my breast cancer journey threw open the doors and windows and tuned me in to the love all around me. That love was in fact a key ingredient to allowing me to come out the other side of my journey more whole and in a sense healthier than ever before.

I hope Charles Schulz will be pleased to know that I am appropriating his structure for my own Love is… piece of poetry.

Love Came to Me Through…
By Diane Davies

Waiting as impatiently as me for the results of tests
Holding me when I awoke screaming from nightmares
Helping me to see who the jackass really was
Waiting for my husband to come home
so as not to leave me alone the
night before surgery
Waiting for my company to leave so he can
come home so I'm not alone the
night before surgery
Nervously driving me to the hospital for the surgery
Hugging me and assuring me of his love before the surgery began
Laughing with me as the pink azaleas took over
my field of vision after the first sedative
Sitting in the waiting room through hours of surgery
Holding my hand in the recovery room
Whispering the "good news" of the can-
cer is gone when I awoke from surgery
Pinching my toe when leaving because every-
thing else hurt too much
Learning how to care for the drain tubes
and then doing it over and over
Moving my healing chair upstairs
Helping me settle in my healing chair
Delivering a warm bowl of homemade wild mushroom soup and a
bouquet of lily of the valley
Getting me a drink of water to take my pills

Plugging in the phone and CD player close to my healing chair
Fluffing my pillows
Washing my hair
Crying with me when the pain was too much to bear
Helping me to take a bath
Waiting outside the bathroom door for my cry of help
Bouquets and more bouquets of fresh flowers
Planters and baskets filled with living plants
Books, cards and letters, phone calls and stop in visits
Wine bottles and a beautiful wine glass
Scrubbing my floors, cleaning my bathrooms, ironing Butch's shirts
Calling in on the phone to remind me not to do too much
Scolding me when I didn't listen
Delivering meals and joining us to enjoy them
Taking me for a ride on a warm sunny day
Don Moen CD – God Will Make a Way
Changing the bedding on our bed
Doing the laundry
Cleaning up the kitchen after a meal
Inviting me to join the Hastings Breast Cancer Support Group
Picking up my prescriptions and a loaf of
bread on the way home from work
Helping me to find the new normal surrounding my new body
Taking me out to lunch when I needed a change of scenery
Bringing in lunch when it was too big a chore for me to go out
Holding my hand in scary times and painful times
Allowing me to grow and change
Making sure I had the time to heal
Listening to me
Listening to me
Listening to me

Chapter 5

Life is a Good and Precious Gift!

> Every morning, when we wake up, we have twen-
> ty-four brand new hours to live. What a precious
> gift! We have the capacity to live in a way that these
> twenty-four hours will bring peace, joy and happi-
> ness to ourselves and others.
>
> —Thick Nhat Hanh

ACCORDING TO OSCAR Wilde, "To live is the rarest thing in
the world. Most people exist, that is all." So what is the difference
between living and existing? I'd like to explore that question a bit
in this chapter. I'm quite certain that I have a lot to learn about the
topic, however, with my limited knowledge and even more so since
my breast cancer experience, I choose to live rather than to just exist.
To exist sounds pretty boring – a plant exists. It has no input into
its life at all. To me to live implies that you not only exist but that
you contribute, influence, and participate in some way. Being open
to the possibilities that life has to offer and making decisions about
what works best for you. I've sensed that when you stop learning

and growing you might just as well stop living as it is then that you just exist.

"Questions about the meaning of life have been expressed in a broad variety of ways, including the following:

1. *What is the meaning of life? What's it all about? Who are we?*
2. *Why are we here? What are we here for?*
3. *What is the origin of life?*
4. *What is the nature of life? What is the nature of reality?*
5. *What is the purpose of life? What is the purpose of one's life?*
6. *What is the significance of life?*
7. *What is meaningful and valuable in life?*
8. *What is the value of life?*
9. *What is the reason to live? What are we living for?*

These questions have resulted in a wide range of competing answers and arguments, from scientific theories, to philosophical, theological, and spiritual explanations. (Wikipedia.org)

My belief is that life is a precious gift and a blessing from our God. Our presence upon this planet is a fleeting thing. Short-lived by any standards. One life-time is just a mere flash in the history of the earth. How seriously, then, ought it to be viewed; how desperately its moments should be treasured. A most disturbing thought is the certainty that we've let life slip away quickly, overlooking so many grand opportunities for advancing ourselves physically, mentally and spiritually as well as occasions for helping others. We can still rescue some of those times by waking in the morning aware of the briefness of our time and the value of the day ahead us. Also we need to take into consideration that this life is a one-time experience. We don't get it to do over again so we are wise to make it count taking nothing for granted. Life on earth is a precious time that we should value. I've often heard that we should do what we love and at the same time love what we do! Seems like wise advice to me.

Sometimes it's easy to stop paying attention to how good our lives are. We go along from day to day with enough food to eat, enough money to pay our bills, and enough activity to keep us happy. Our comfort level is high and we tend to forget that not everyone has even these basic things. We become used to our standard of living and the things that make our life run smoothly. Often it is a serious event or situation in our lives that wakes us up to the understanding of what we truly have. In my life, it was my husband's stroke and my breast cancer that shook the foundation. Recently we've had a number of good friends that have passed away; suicide, pancreatic cancer, breast cancer, heart attack, accidents, to name a few of the causes. More and more of our friends are being diagnosed with early onset Alzheimer's and/or dementia. When we are faced with these kinds of events and must persevere, we come to a new understanding of what it is that we have and gain a new lease on life and a new gratefulness regarding our own situation.

Just what is a new lease on life? Well for example my healing chair was beginning to look old and a bit dirty so I had it re-covered in fresh fabric. It now looks better and blends more agreeably with my new décor. I could say it has a new lease on life. After a period of illness or sadness, if something makes you happy or healthy or gives you new energy and enthusiasm, it could be said that you have a new lease on life. In my case, I'd like the definition to be even stronger. If an event or situation is attitude changing or even life-changing, it can be said to give you a new lease on life. The world then looks different. Possibilities come into view that you did not or could not see before. The people in your life become more important to you and you want to let them know how you feel. With a new lease on life, you might decide to make big changes in how you spend your time and whom you see. It's about making better choices and living one's best life.

Breast cancer gave me the opportunity to consider my own impermanence on this earth. Hearing the words, "You have breast cancer" lead me directly to planning my funeral without giving ear to what the doctor was saying about treatment possibilities. My mind could not take it all in beyond the cancer word death sentence. Through my advocacy with other breast cancer patients, I've observed that this state of mind is not uncommon. Having had a glimpse of that reality for myself, has helped me to gain back my life with some major changes for a better way of living.

Love and relationships have taken on more meaning and have moved to the highest priority. The realization that the time table stops for no one and no thing adds even more significance to that statement. My job and job related activities at one point in time held that urgency. If love and relationships are not nurtured and cared for they will look elsewhere for what they need. Fortunately for me, I realized that in time. My husband and family hold the highest importance and bring me the greatest joy.

At the beginning of my breast cancer journey before I had an idea of what my outcome may be, I mourned the fact that I did not have any grandchildren. I was afraid that another woman would have the pleasure of hearing my future grandchildren call her grandma in my place. I was jealous. Children to me are one of life's greatest treasures and I was about to be cheated out of the experience of being a grandparent. As a three-year cancer survivor, my daughter and her husband blessed me with a beautiful granddaughter. Five years later another blessing in my grandson. Oh life is so good. I've now discovered what a joy being a grandparent can be. There is no better feeling than having those little arms hugging you around the neck or tiny lips smothering your face in sloppy wet kisses. There is such joy in receiving and eating a fuzzy old M&M from the pocket of a grand child saved especially for you with love. They grow up way too fast but I persist in finding new delight in each stage of their development. My hope is that I will be able to continue to watch their growth for many years to come.

Having our grandchildren living next door presents many opportunities to spend quality time together. One of the things I love is viewing live theatre productions. With The Children's Theatre Company in Minneapolis, we have a marvelous opportunity to nurture the love of theatre in our children at a young age. A few years ago when Elsie was four or five, I took my daughter and granddaughter to see the Children's Theatre production of Annie. Thirty years ago my mother and I did the same with my daughter so I was pretty excited to be repeating the opportunity with the next generation. Elsie loved the characters and the music and the colorful costuming until Rooster (the villain as you will remember) came onto the stage. She was so scared that she wanted to go home immediately! Tears filled her eyes as she jumped up in my lap and held on for dear life. As I thought about it, stories and movies are one thing. I could explain that it was just pretend and not really happening. But here we were "live and in person" with a villain running around on the stage. "I can see him and he is right there and he is scary!", she responded. It took a while in the crying room watching the production on closed circuit TV before she calmed down and could enjoy the rest of the story. She still is not too excited about being scared but she does understand the difference between reality and make believe. Oh the lessons we learn as parents and grandparents. I'm so blessed not to have missed these opportunities in my life.

I quickly jumped into the shower knowing that Elsie and Eli were due home from school and preschool at any time. They usually stop in daily for a visit with "Gram, Gram" and "Papa" before heading back home for dinner and bedtime. I heard the home security system chime telling me that an outside door had just opened and closed. Then I heard the sound of little feet running down the hallway heading for my bedroom and bathroom. Realizing I was about to be caught naked in the shower, I had no way to stop the inevitable. It was even to late to grab for my towel. The little three-year-old face of my Eli peeked around the corner of the shower. He was surprised to see his Gram Gram in all her splendid naked glory. His gaze slowly traveled the length of my body from head to toe and back to head once again. I could only imagine what kind of comment I was about to hear. With a twinkle in his eyes and his devilish grin, he looked up at me and said, "Gram Gram, how come you belly stick out like that?" My reply, "Come here you little stinker. I think I'm going to drown you." Off he went giggling his way back down the hallway to wait for me to get dressed and join him for our hour or so together. I just never know what to expect from him but that is the joy of grandparent hood.

One more story – Memorial weekend Butch and I flew our De Havilland Beaver to our cabin on Rainy Lake in Ontario, Canada where we parked the airplane on the beach. When Krisi and Jeff and the kids arrived in Fort Frances, Papa flew in to pick them up. Now remember this is late May in Canada and it is not exactly warm. After unloading the airplane, Eli climbed back up on the floats and jumped into the lake. Not to be outdone, Elsie did the same. With screams and giggles of delight the two of them played in the water for a good hour or so in spite of bright red legs and purple lips from the cold. How do you stop a seven and three-year old from playing in the water after a long Minnesota winter? Warm towels and dry clothes did the trick of warming them up along with a bit of cuddling with Grandma and Mommy when the swimming was done. Without my new lease on life I could have missed out on all of this love!

My faith now plays a greater role in my life. I believe more strongly in the importance of a relationship with our creator as well as in the power of prayer. A good friend of mine was diagnosed three years ago with pancreatic cancer. Her mantra became Psalm 46:10, "Be still and know that I am God." Her strong faith and love for her family gave her another three years of life that is unheard of for that kind of diagnosis. She became my role model for dying with grace and dignity.

An attribute that I have always coveted is patience. Teaching first grade for sixteen years should attest to the fact that I do have patience. However, patience includes the capacity to accept or tolerate delay, trouble or suffering without getting angry or upset and it demands a certain amount of calmness, composure and peace as well. My breast cancer journey afforded me numerous opportunities to practice this characteristic. I do believe that now, on this side of cancer, I am more patient than ever. I stay much calmer and find that little things certainly do not rattle me as much as before. My husband and I purchased a 2015 50th Anniversary Ford Mustang with all the bells and whistles including the standard transmission with six speeds. Many years ago when learning how to drive, my dad insisted that I learn in and take my driver's test in a standard transmission. That resulted in my having to take the driver's test several times but I did learn how to use the clutch, park on hills and basically master shifting. Now here I am relearning and practicing those skills. I'm doing pretty well, keeping calm, and only jerking now and then. Traffic continues to make me a bit nervous but to show you how far I've come in my six hundred miles or so of practice I'll share this with you. Crossing a busy intersection found me in first gear at the stop sign. When it was my turn, I carefully let out the clutch and chugged into the intersection before I killed the motor. I restarted the car and chugged and jerked another couple of feet before killing it once again. Not knowing what else to do, I just laughed and waved at the waiting traffic. Started the car again and finally made it through the intersection. That does not happen too often any more but when it does I just take a deep breath and continue on. It especially makes me smile when my husband chugs and jerks now and then. Hey, we all make mistakes – right? After all that is what I taught my first graders every day – we all make mistakes and we learn from those mistakes. I've learned to go easy on myself and that is okay!

Many of us are familiar with the expression, "When God closes a door he opens a window." Sometimes, though, he doesn't just open a window, he rips the roof right off what we thought was possible, making way for something far better. (Meadow Linn) My breast cancer journey certainly ripped the roof right off of my life and made room for something better. When my Mom was recovering from her cancer journey in the early 70's, she went through a period of depression. My advice to her was to volunteer and help others on their journeys. Thirty years later my words to her began to echo in my own head. Little did I know the places my volunteering would take me and the things that I would find myself doing. I share this with you not to brag and boast but to show you the possibilities that exist out there and perhaps inspire your own volunteerism.

One of my first ventures into reaching out to others was through the American Cancer Society Reach to Recovery Program. This program matches breast cancer survivors with newly diagnosed patients having similar backgrounds and diagnosis. As a volunteer at that time, we met directly with the patient either at their home or in a restaurant or coffee shop. This one to one, face to face experience I found the most rewarding. I remember knocking at the door and seeing a frightened tearful face appear to allow me into her home and life. I'd break the ice by talking a bit about my own breast cancer journey and then slowly begin to ask a few questions to help my new friend relax into the safety of our conversation. After a while I'd offer to share my scars remembering how I wondered what I'd look like after surgery. Nine times out of ten, they would take me up on my offer. Their next question would be, "May I touch it?" For many this would be their first experience with seeing a silicone implant embedded under skin. After shedding a few tears together, a touching of my scars and implants and finally a hug, I would see that face of fear begin to soften into a smile and finally a new look of determination and courage. Unfortunately today's Reach to Recovery visits are made over the telephone. I'm sure the results are still positive but certainly lacking without the personal touch.

Through my volunteering with ACS, I became an ambassador for Minnesota to the Relay for Life celebration in Washington D.C. called the Celebration on the Hill. We not only participated in the relay in front of our nation's capitol, but also visited with our state's senators and representatives in prearranged interviews for the purpose of sharing our cancer experiences. Each state brought Banners of Hope signed by constituents back home. These banners became a temporary Wall of Hope in front of the Washington Monument the evening of the event. With tears streaming down our faces and high fives coming from bystanders, we survivors took the first lap around the reflecting pool to the cheers of the thousands ready to walk for hope. I call that my one and only "rock star" appearance.

Back home in Minnesota, I have been the guest speaker starting the Relay for Life celebration in Hastings and the Making Strides Against Breast Cancer Walk around Lake Nokomis in Minneapolis. I've been happy to participate in a few other relays in the area including one in River Falls, WI. where I played a role in getting their breast cancer support group up and running. The first lap at these events is always for those having survived a cancer journey and always brings on the chills and tears from me and hundreds of others.

My first book, ***From There to Here***, brought many opportunities into my life. I made author visits to several bookstores in the area with the largest being at the Just Thinking bookstore in Hastings. My book was responsible for newspaper articles and an appearance in the St. Croix Valley Magazine. I was even interviewed on talk radio. Guest speaking invitations took me to Lakeview Hospital in Stillwater, MN where I spoke to an early morning meeting of First Rounds for the medical staff and several afternoon and evening meetings with their breast cancer support group. The American Association of University Women (AAUW) invited me to appear at the 3M Center in St. Paul's meeting as well as the group gathering in Hastings. I have also spoken at several churches in the area including my home church in Cottage Grove.

Early on at the urging of a friend, I attended a meeting of the Hastings Breast Cancer Support Group (HBCSG - www.hastings-breastcancer.com). I went with the attitude that I would visit one meeting to satisfy my friend and found camaraderie, friendship and hope beyond what I had ever expected. To give you an idea of the amity of the group, here is an excerpt from their brochure:

> **About the Hastings Breast Cancer Support Group**– The Hastings Breast Cancer Support Group is an organization dedicated to offering support in a safe environment where you can question and seek

answers, laugh and cry, share your concerns, and grow in knowledge, understanding and compassion. Most of all we do offer HOPE! Your own hope will grow as you meet women of all ages who are newly diagnosed, who are now undergoing treatment, who have lived with their illness for years and even those who are considered cured. We all have one thing in common; we see each day as a precious gift to be lived to the fullest. Providing education and support to the newly diagnosed on both a local and national basis through our support materials including our two Voices of Hope DVDs is one of our primary missions. As a support group, we offer no magic pill that will take away your personal pain. We do offer understanding; because each of us has made the journey you may now be walking.

I'm still a member to this day. I took on the co-leader position for several years and then became the project director for the Voices of Hope DVD series. The DVD series provides hope and emotional encouragement for newly diagnosed breast cancer patients and their caregivers through a virtual support group. (www.voicesofhope.com) This series became our answer to "How do we reach out with peer support to the newly diagnosed?" Many of the members of our support group were bravely interviewed along with their caregivers to appear in this series. Ten of the twelve participants discreetly show the audience their scars and talk about the surgeries and reconstruction that they underwent as a special feature of the DVD. As this was something that we all wished we could have experienced before our own surgeries, it became a priority to be included in the series. The Cancer Patient Education Network (CPEN), an international network for patient educators, awarded HBCSG with their 2013 Award for Excellence in Education at their annual meeting and conference in Seattle, WA. The series has enjoyed tremendous success and has brought us to several seminars and conferences. The Minnesota Lynx women's professional basketball team foundation presented HBCSG with a grant check at center court during a season game halftime.

You of course realize that all of these activities don't just fall out of the sky and into your lap. It takes planning, determination, and courage that all bring a special reward to the grateful soul. In my kitchen, I have a wooden plate displayed that reads; "Life is not waiting for the storm to pass, it is learning how to dance in the rain." I have danced in the rain and hope to continue dancing for many years to come.

Chapter 6

Gifts of Gratitude

"Be thankful for what you have; you'll end up having
more. If you concentrate on what you don't have,
you will never, ever have enough."

—Oprah Winfrey

"GRATITUDE IS NOT only the greatest of virtues, but the parent of all others." Cicero (106– 43 BCE) Cicero lived a really really long time ago in ancient Rome. He was a philosopher, politician, lawyer, orator, political theorist, consul and constitutionalist. He came from a wealthy family of the Roman equestrian order, and is widely considered one of Rome's greatest orators and prose stylists. He lived in the times just before the birth of Christ. We understand from this quote the high regard he had for gratitude.

A virtue is an admirable quality, an asset, or an advantage. In othe words it is a good thing to have. Isn't it interesting to realize that even in ancient times well over 2000 years ago gratitude was recognized as an important asset to possess? We're still talking about it and still comprehending the power that it exhibits and still seeking to live by it today.

Melody Beattie says it this way; "Gratitude unlocks the fullness of life. It turns what we have into enough, and more. It turns denial into acceptance, chaos to order, and confusion to clarity. It can turn a meal into a feast, a house into a home, a stranger into a friend." Now that is certainly powerful.

In 1999, a group of women from our church began to study gratitude through the use of *Simple Abundance; A Daybook of Comfort and Joy* by Sarah Ban Breathnach. The author suggests keeping a daily gratitude journal in which you write five things each day that you are thankful for. One catch is that you cannot make any repeats. This is an interesting thing to do if you have never tried it. It does help point out all of the abundance we enjoy in our lives. As we studied, we began to realize that are very rich women. Rich in the sense that we began to "open the eyes of our eyes" and see that our basic needs were being met. As we began to focus on the abundance rather than the lack in our lives, we experienced a sense of fulfillment, which is gratitude at work. The natural outcome that gratitude brings is the desire to share what we have with others, to reach out with love and thanksgiving to those around us. The Gratitude Group is still meeting nearly sixteen years since our journey began. The emphasis is now completely on helping others with many projects for the benefit of all ages.

The study of gratitude left this group of women and myself with a long list of lessons learned. As our study continued, our list continued to grow. Allow me to share that list with you:

Gratitude…

- Helps keep us young. If we fail to grow, the light inside each of us grows dim.
- Makes us feel good. It works like mental sunshine. It is a choice we make that leads to happiness.

- Creates happiness because it makes us feel full and complete. Gratitude and joy are inseparable.
- Is the realization that we have everything we need at the moment.
- Opens us up to the magic and beauty of life.
- Promotes health. Believe it or not endorphins are natural painkillers.
- Eradicates worry. Worry happens when we focus on the future. Gratitude demands that we focus on the here and now and become engrossed in the present moment.
- Melts away fear, anger and bitterness as we focus on what we are thankful for.
- Draws people to us. When we are grateful, we radiate happiness, which in turn acts like a magnet for others.
- Antidote to bitterness and resentment as we begin to tap into the experience of the abundance in our lives.
- Cures perfectionism by helping us widen our frame of vision. We are no longer looking for what's wrong but rather what is right by tracking success.
- Releases us from the "gimmes" as we focus on all the wonderful things already happening in our day-to-day lives.
- Keeps us current.
- Opens our hearts.
- Generates kindness and generosity. The more you give the more you get.
- Joins us to life.
- Connects us to spirit.
- Opens us to moments of grace when we tap into the fullness of a sense of thankfulness.
- Helps us live in joyful expectation and look for hidden blessings in difficult situations.

Attitudes of Gratitude: How to Give and Receive Joy Every Day... by M.J. Ryan is an inspiring book that shows us how to rejoice in what we have and live each day to it's fullest! Sound familiar? "Gratitude births only positive feelings – love, compassion, joy, and hope. As we focus on what we are thankful for, fear, anger, and bitterness simply melt away, seemingly without effort." Ryan believes that gratitude is both an attitude and a practice. An attitude of gratitude requires being put into action where it will create a strong resonance between our thoughts and our actions. Ryan lays out twenty-six different practices to help us live with this "great fullness" in our lives. The list of practices are Ryan's and the comments are mine.

Exercise Daily – to build a muscle or an attitude you must practice using it daily.

Choose Gratefulness "In Spite Of…" – We cannot wait for everything to be okay before we choose happiness or joy. We must catch it as it passes even if it comes in the midst of sorrow or suffering – maybe even especially then. Not that we deny the suffering, but not let it blind us to the beauty and joy that is there too at the same time.

Revel in the Ordinary – Celebrate the normal, the commonplace, and the regular things of life. If all we have to put on the hotdogs is catsup, celebrate that fact and not bemoan that we have no mustard or relish.

What Do You Really Need – "The grand essentials in life are something to do, something to love, and something to hope for." Joseph Addison Take a look around at all that you do have and acknowledge that. Always looking for more only adds to the discontent. Why would we want to focus on that? Joy, happiness, optimism, faith and trust are there for us. What more do we really need?

Do the Work of Forgiveness – Anger and resentment block the feelings of gratitude. We can't feel grateful or receive the gifts of joy when we feel hurt, angry or sorrowful. We cannot force ourselves to feel grateful with such strong negative feelings. Only forgiveness can help us move on. Ryan suggests a practice called "The Damage Report" where you write a letter (that you never send) to your abuser detailing the effects the wounding had on you. Don't hold back. Then set up a boundary; I will get up and leave the room if someone is verbally abusing me, or whatever the case may be. Then write a note of forgiveness to yourself for not having stated your boundary before. Finally write a note of thanks to the other person for the learning, so that it won't happen again. Taking the time to really express your needs and pains and state your boundary, you'll begin to be grateful for the lessons the wounding caused you to learn. Forgiveness leads to gratitude in a healing movement.

Practice Wonderment – amazement, awe, and surprise! Children are our greatest teachers of wonderment. We seem to lose our joy, our exuberance, and our passionate embrace of life as we grow up. We need to open our senses and let the world come in anew.

Don't Compare – "Life begets life. Energy creates energy. It is by spending oneself that one becomes rich." Sarah Bernhardt Don't be continually looking over the fence at what the neighbor has. His needs are different than yours. Being grateful lights up what we already have.

Transform Expectations into No Matter Whats – Expectations are the killers of gratitude and joy. They can create blinders so that we can't see the true blessings of our lives. All that we have becomes invisible because it somehow doesn't match the picture of what is expected. When we look outside of ourselves for happiness, we lose our power. We can't count on anything but ourselves for our own happiness. We each have the ability to choose how we will respond to what happens to us and what we will focus on to make us happy. Before I would get out of bed in the morning during my breast cancer journey and still now twelve years later, I make the decision about how my day will go. Will I be a victim or a survivor? So much more joy and happiness can be found by choosing to be the survivor.

Develop of Good Memory – Create a large backup supply of contentment and joyful memories to carry you through tough times. Not all days are going to be good. We all know that. Having this backup supply of good times and good memories is wonderful to fall back on when times get hard.

Take Time to Smell the Roses – You need to slow down long enough to notice what is right in front of your nose. When suffering from this "no time syndrome", I try and ask myself what would be the worst that could happen if I don't meet the deadline or make the appointment? And I can usually now talk myself into taking more time smelling the roses, being with the grandchildren, making time for my husband and his needs and wants.

Focus on What's Right – We are well trained to look at what's wrong and overlook what's right. We have it backwards according to Ryan. Instead of commenting on a mistake that someone you live with made, try complimenting him or her on something that went right. It can change a day or even an attitude.

Be Willing to Embrace What Shows Up – "I have learned, in whatsoever state I am in, therewith to be content." Saint Paul When we are grateful for what is, we experience contentment. Contentment with what is makes us happy in the moment and available for whatever life has in store for us. The old saying about taking lemons and making lemonade comes to mind. Twelve years out from my reconstruction surgery, I find that I have gained a bit of weight. I was explaining to a friend the other day how because of that weight I now have four boobs – my two silicone ones made by the implants and the two new ones that have appeared under my arms made by my new fat. It is really okay – I'm still here to laugh about it and do something about it if I really want to make a change. My husband always has said that he likes his woman to have a little meat on her bones. That she does!

Say Thank You as Often as Possible – Wouldn't the world be a better place if we all did this? Try it out sometime. You'll be amazed at what a difference a smile and a thank you can make in the grocery line, or purchasing gas, or whatever errand it is that you have to run. There is nothing wrong with a little pleasantness in life. I've found that it even makes me feel better.

Leave a Trail of Happiness – Try living every day as if it were your last. I'd much rather be remembered with a smile and a polite thank you than as a bitter old curmudgeon. One day at Sam's Club I noticed an older gentleman behind me in line that had quite a scowl on his face. He had about three things in his cart and mine was full to over-flowing. I would have let him go ahead of me but I didn't notice him until the clerk was already ringing up my order. I told her to add his things to my bill. After her incredulous look, she did as I asked. Her smile was bigger than mine when she told the irritable guy that I had already paid for his items. When he waved and smiled my way, he looked ten years younger. I wonder what he told his wife when he arrived home. I think my little act of kindness was a real day bright-ener for him. Give it a try. It was a fun little experiment.

Write a Thank You to Yourself – Why not? Give yourself thanks and credit for all you do. It is nice to be appreciated so why not do the appreciating?

Fall in Love Again and Again – This does not just mean your spouse but that would be fun and exciting. You can fall in love with any number of things; a new book, a new look, a new practice or attitude.

Appreciate Your Kids Just As They Are – whether they are just little kids or the all grown up kind of adult kids. Appreciate can mean to value somebody or something highly, or understand something, or feel gratitude regarding or even increase in value. Our kids do all of these things and giving a little appreciation may just go a long way in their life as well.

Live as if Every Day Is Your Last – My hope is that when my last day comes I can live it with the realization of my own self-worth, contentment with knowing that the living of my life has left the world a little bit better, and that my gratefulness for a good life has been expressed.

Being a Gracious Receiver

"When we give cheerfully and accept gratefully,
everyone is blessed."

—Maya Angelou

NEWLY HOME FROM the hospital after my breast cancer surgery, I remember sitting in my healing chair as my Gratitude Group from church cleaned my house as a gift for me. They vacuumed, dusted, ironed, scrubbed bathrooms, washed our clothes as well as cleaned my floors. As an extra special treatment, they brought a lovely bouquet of flowers and a delicious lunch. From my chair, I cried tears of thankfulness, joy and love. Mixed in with all of that I also felt a touch of discomfort. Being the one who always did for others, I found it difficult to be on the receiving end. They taught me that being a gracious receiver is important as it allowed them to do something for me taking away their helpless feeling in the face of my breast cancer.

As a result of that experience, I've been doing some research and experimenting with this idea of being a gracious receiver. We've all heard the cliché, "It's better to give than to receive." In fact we were probably even taught that by our parents/guardians and our church or even taught it ourselves to our own children. I have found that it is even easier to give than to receive. Remember that discomfort I was feeling as my friends cleaned for me? That discomfort could even be described as painfully difficult, awkward, humbling and embarrassing. That's the hard part of receiving. It is not easy to admit that we need help and by accepting that help we feel rather naked and stripped of our dignity. We may even feel indebtedness.

So how do we overcome these feelings and learn to be a gracious receiver? I'm trying. One of the first ways I've experimented with is to say a simple thank you when someone gives me a compliment. For example, when someone says, "I love that outfit you have on," in the past I may have replied with something like, "Oh I dug to the back of my closet and there it was." Or "I found it at Target". Or "You don't think it makes me look fat?" Sounds pretty condescending or superior doesn't it? Why should I protest being given a gift? A simple thank you would have been much better.

In my reading I came across a story of a young girl who received a beading set as a Christmas gift. She was thrilled and expressed her gratitude to the giver of the gift. Her mother suggested that she make a bracelet with the beads and choose someone at the party to give it to. Excited to please her mother she chose her great aunt who was sitting off to the side of everyone else looking rather pinched face and sad. The great aunt picked up the bracelet with her thumb and forefinger as if it was something disgusting and foul and dropped it back into the small hands of the giver without even so much as a smile or a nod. Her insensitive reaction broke the heart of the little girl. As I read and reread this story, I began to realize that when I refuse to accept a gift or downplay a compliment I am reacting the same as the great aunt breaking the heart of the giver. Every gift is an opportunity to build or strengthen the bond of love and that love and the relationship it represents is the most important piece over and above the gift given.

James 1:17 tells us "That every good and perfect gift is from above." The giver of all good is God even if His divine love uses other people in our life to make the gift happen. Receiving is equally as important as giving. If all were the givers, who would be there to receive? I believe in the existence of a giving cycle that we have the responsibility to keep going. If we don't receive, we cut our self from the process and the strengthening of the bond of love doing ourselves harm. "By being open to receive, you actually create an abundance cycle that allows you to receive even more. Think of clinched fists. If you go through life with clenched fists, you can't grasp or hold on to anything new that comes your way. However, if your hands are open, you are able to receive whatever is presented to you. You're opening yourself to the abundance of the universe." Suzanne Fetting

Suzanne Fetting, Confidence Coach in Vancouver B.C., gives us a few tips for becoming a more gracious receiver: (absoluteconfidence.com)

1. **Eliminate your limiting beliefs**
   If you lack self-worth and have limiting beliefs about receiving it can be difficult for you to receive. Let others do kind things for you, you do deserve it!
   It IS a myth that if you get more, someone else gets less. There is more than enough in the universe to go around. And you do deserve all the wonderful things you receive in life.

2. **Learn to say, *"Thank you."***
   Never, ever say, *"Oh! You shouldn't have."* It makes the giver feel as if they shouldn't have bothered giving you a gift and it gives the impression that you don't appreciate the gift.
   It makes the giver feel great to give gifts. How do you feel when you give to others? Good, right? You will find that you enjoy receiving more when you just accept it with gratitude.

3. **Stay open to receiving**
The next time someone offers to do you a favor or pay for lunch or help you out in some way, let them. The more open you are the more that will come to you. As you become a better receiver, you will naturally become a better giver. Stay open and grateful to receiving and your gratitude will bring more gifts to you.

Remember, a giver must have a receiver. Being a gracious receiver is a gift you can give to the giver. Enjoying what you receive is an expression of gratitude. Start letting others give to you and be happy and grateful when accepting their gifts. I read somewhere that we should treat every gift like a treasure with enthusiasm and grace and make it a good experience for the giver. We can try saying in a genuine authentic way things like; I really appreciate this, thank you so much, that was very kind of you, what a blessing this is to me so as not to dismiss the act of giving.

"It's not about the love I get… It's about the love I give!" says Charles Schulz using the voice of our good friend, Snoopy. Being a gracious receiver is a good way to spread that love.

Chapter 8

Lifesavers – Listen and Trust

We're never so vulnerable than when we trust someone - but paradoxically, if we cannot trust, neither
can we find love or joy.

—Walter Anderson

WHEN I HEAR the words lifesaver I think of the little round tube shaped colored candies that come in roll. Red has always been my favorite. I loved them as a kid and still do today. The Merriam-Webster Dictionary defines lifesaver: as something that saves a person's life (duh!): a personal flotation device: something or someone, which provides help that is badly needed. As I'm sure you've guessed, the final definition is the topic of this segment.

In the late 80's, my husband purchased our first airplane. He had his pilot's license before he even had a driver's license so the purchase came as no surprise to me. We discussed the idea that I should also take some flying lessons and eventually get my pilot's license as well. I started those lessons at the St. Paul Downtown Airport shortly thereafter with my friends teasing me about being sure to leave the huge number one on top of the 1ˢᵗ National Bank Building that appears not too far off of the runway.

My first clue that perhaps this flying stuff was not for me was when I'd wake up on a lesson morning and find myself hoping for bad weather so as not to have to fly. I had a few hours under my belt and knew that I was getting close to my first solo flight, which scared me to death. These are not the thoughts of someone that is in love with flying. During my last lesson, it started to rain. My instructor and I were about finished for the day and were third in line to land. On the radio I heard the call letters of the plane I was flying with the instructions to take an immediate one eighty to the right because of some unknown traffic in the pattern. One eighty is a 90 degree turn to the right which I did. I then took my hands and feet off of the controls and said, "I'm done. You can land it." My instructor took over with ease and before I knew it we were on the ground. We were really in no danger. The danger was only in my mind. "Are you taxiing in or do I have to do that too?" I heard from my right. After I parked the plane, we sat for a while in silence in the sweltering heat inside the plane. My lifesaver/instructor (someone who provides help when badly needed) talked me out of my fright. He explained that if I really wanted to learn to fly I had to put my trust in him and let him teach me. That was an extremely difficult assignment for me to carry out. I'm the one in charge and I have a real problem giving up that control. As I said, that was my final lesson. I love to fly with my husband as the pilot but don't ask me to take over any controls.

During my breast cancer journey, I was forced to give over control of my body to my medical team. I had no choice in the matter if I wanted to survive. Much later into the journey when the living/dying question had been answered for the time being, I was getting close to the end of the expansion period of my reconstruction. The expanders under my chest muscles had been filled with saline solution to the size I wanted my breasts to be. It was now a matter of waiting for three months to insure that a pocket was formed to hold the implants in place. The plastic surgeon suggested that I try on bras, swimming suits, and different styles of clothing to make sure that I was happy with my new size. "We can still change the size while the expanders are in," he explained. "But once the implants are in place, there is no going upward or downward in size." Once again, I failed to give up my control to a lifesaver/instructor. I thought I knew what size I wanted my body to be so I did not do as he suggested.

When the implants were in and healed, I went to a mastectomy fitter to purchase bras and discovered that I was between sizes. I would have known this had I listened to my surgeon in the first place. I was fitted with a prosthesis piece to wear under my bra to add about a quarter of an inch to my breast size. I found it heavy and warm and uncomfortable to wear. Sometimes it is best if I do listen and trust that others do know what they are talking about and follow their advice.

Another lifesaver/instructor came to me by the name of Marisha. We met through an author event celebrating the writers and their books from the Hastings area. Our book tables were set up appropriately in the library of the Historic LuDuc Mansion in Hastings, MN. We chatted a bit about our books and our lives and felt instantly drawn together by our ideas and our missions. In response to Marisha's question regarding what was next for me, I explained to her how my breast cancer support group was actively raising money to put together a DVD for women newly diagnosed with breast cancer. "I can help you with that. I've done some film work and would be happy to work with you on this project," came Marisha's response and the beginning of a friendship and partnership that helped me learn and grow on many levels. As a result of this encounter, Voices of Hope DVD series became a reality. I've included a press release regarding the series to tell you more about the project:

"Voices of Hope" DVD Series Provides Breast Cancer Patients with Hope and Encouragement

November 20, 2013

You've just been diagnosed with breast cancer—now what? This diagnosis can be a terrifying moment – a time of isolation, confusion and despair. You feel overwhelmed, even panicked and fearful, and have probably found the clinical "next step" information confusing at best. Most importantly, the decisions that you make now may directly affect the outcome of your care. The *Voices of Hope* DVD series features a diverse group of women and men who have personally experienced breast cancer and offers help to empower the newly diagnosed with hope, inspiration and important information that can help them navigate the critical first weeks from diagnosis to treatment.

Voices of Hope DVD series is an outreach project of The Hastings Breast Cancer Support Group of Hastings, Minnesota. Its inspiration stems from the recognition that a powerful and often neglected source of breast cancer expertise is the peer group – women and men who have experienced the challenges of this disease firsthand. Inspired by the stories of these brave patient's, Hastings Breast Cancer Support Group saw an opportunity to spread this wisdom beyond the boundaries of their local support group. In 2010, the original *Voices of Hope* DVD was created to provide a virtual breast cancer support group that would help other breast cancer patients navigate the early weeks of breast cancer treatment, from diagnosis to first plans of action. ***Voices of Hope*** does not offer medical advice in any way. It was designed to offer comfort, support and hope for patients newly diagnosed and the people who love them. In the "Special Feature", as listed on the DVD menu, ten of the twelve women interviewed display their scars and talk about the type of procedures they experienced. Clinics and cancer care centers find this invaluable when working with new patients. The positive responses to this video have been overwhelming, with thousands of copies now circulating throughout the United States and Canada.

Based on feedback received from patients, medical professionals, and friends and family members of breast cancer patients who viewed Voices of Hope, a second documentary was created, ***Voices of Hope: Family and Friends***. Loved ones of breast cancer patients often have no idea how to help, what to say, and how to calm their own fears. Voices of Hope: Family and Friends focuses on the healing power of relationships and features breast cancer patients and their family and friends who reflect on their journey, creating a positive mindset for each viewer that leads to better medical outcomes and a stronger social network. This well-received DVD focuses on the stories of spouses, partners, children, friends, and others who have supported breast cancer patients throughout their journey. Both newly diagnosed and friends and family members of breast cancer patients have found this new DVD to be a vital source of comfort and education.

Contact

To learn more the Voices of Hope Series and the Hastings Breast Cancer Support Group, please visit our website at www.voicesofhopebc.com or contact: Claire Mathews at Claire.mathews55@gmail.com

I do believe that people come into our lives for a reason, a season or a lifetime and their being there is not a coincidence but all part of a plan to help us understand our mission here on earth. Marisha was one of those people in my life that came for a reason. Perhaps this poem will help you identify with what I am saying.

Reason, Season, Lifetime
Author Unknown

People come into your life for a reason, a season or a lifetime.

When you figure out which one it is,
you will know what to do for each person.

When someone is in your life for a REASON,
it is usually to meet a need you have expressed.
They have come to assist you through a difficulty;
to provide you with guidance and support;
to aid you physically, emotionally or spiritually.
They may seem like a godsend, and they are.
They are there for the reason you need them to be.

Then, without any wrongdoing on your
part or at an inconvenient time,
this person will say or do something to bring the relationship to an end.
Sometimes they die. Sometimes they walk away.
Sometimes they act up and force you to take a stand.
What we must realize is that our need has been met, our
desire fulfilled; their work is done. The prayer you sent up
has been answered and now it is time to move on.

Some people come into your life for a SEASON,
because your turn has come to share, grow or learn.
They bring you an experience of peace or make you laugh.
They may teach you something you have never done.
They usually give you an unbelievable amount of joy.
Believe it. It is real. But only for a season.

LIFETIME relationships teach you lifetime lessons;
things you must build upon in order to have
a solid emotional foundation.
Your job is to accept the lesson, love the person,
and put what you have learned to use in all other
relationships and areas of your life.
It is said that love is blind but friendship is clairvoyant.

Marisha came into my life to share my dream and help the Hastings Breast Cancer Support Group make **Voices of Hope** a reality. We made some great progress moving peer support for breast cancer patients forward a bit and perhaps into the light. She empowered me both professionally and personally through our working relationship and just as importantly through our friendship. In 2011, I was awarded a Bush Fellowship by means of Marisha's help. She not only was the impetus for the nomination but also the stimulus for creating within me the self-confidence to achieve the fellowship. A part of my nomination process was to write a plan explaining what the work of my fellowship would be, what community I would be working to make a difference in, and how I planned to use the dollars that came with the fellowship. The next step to receiving the award was a four-hour interview with four teams of judges covering my application materials. Marisha and I together crafted the materials and wrote possible questions that would be covered in the interview along with their answers. Then we practiced until I knew the material backwards, forewords and upside-down. The preparation paid off as I was awarded the Bush Fellowship for 2011–2013.

The Bush Foundation was formed in 1953. The organization awards $40 million a year to philanthropic organizations primarily located in Minnesota and the Upper Midwest. The mission of the Bush Foundation is to be a catalyst for the courageous leadership necessary to create sustainable solutions to tough public problems and ensure community vitality. My organization was the Hastings Breast Cancer Support Group. The community served was breast cancer survivors. My work was lightening the load of the newly diagnosed breast cancer patient through the power of peer support offering emotional encouragement and providing hope. The creation of the second DVD in the Voices of Hope series was an accomplishment of the fellowship.

Being a part of a Bush cohort for a little over two years was truly an amazing experience and was responsible for my largest growth in leadership skills in my life so far. It was hard work but then isn't that true of all growth that we achieve? "No pain, no gain," as I have often heard. The week before the first seminar I was diagnosed with shingles. I'm pretty sure it was my apprehension and stress over the coming fellowship mixed with my dormant chickenpox virus that caused the outbreak and the pain. I'd rather go through my double mastectomy again than experience another occurrence of shingles.

Our cohort met for two-day leadership training seminars twelve times during the two-year period. As I discovered the Bush Fellowship was more about helping me become the best leader possible to accomplish my mission or my "work" as we described it. I do see **myself** differently now and more clearly. I've found more confidence in the power of Diane Davies as a leader. Somewhere around January of 2012 after sharing with the cohort my lack of guts to make a change that I knew I needed to make, and while working with my coach, I came to the realization that **it was and is me**. I can and do make a difference in the lives of many around me. With the help of these Fellowship seminars and my own desire to do the tough work that it takes to grow, I came to realize the importance of being authentic and straightforward with myself. When I do that my leadership becomes more authentic and straightforward

The dilemma that was responsible for my biggest steps forward as a leader was the very dilemma that was almost responsible for causing me to throw in the towel. That quandary was my decision to dissolve my connection with the nonprofit, Circle in the Field: Peer Support for Breast Cancer, which Marisha and I had so recently created. It forced me to confront my experienced mentor and friend, Marisha. Confrontation is still an area that I have trouble with even into my sixties. My parents were good people and did many good things for our family and our community but I cannot think of a time when I saw them role model for me how to navigate through differences of opinion – how to do battle. So I learned how to avoid confrontation, how to placate and satisfy no matter what the cost to me. At the time of my diagnosis with breast cancer, I would have given anything to be able to find an escape route that would enable me to bypass what lay ahead. I felt the same way once again in this instance. I knew I had to face into the storm and cross that mountain. I also knew that I had to do it for myself and by myself. Brutal honesty, harsh criticism, tears of anguish and despair pushed me forward. At the end of the long night comes the peacefulness of the new day. With lessons learned regarding unclear expectations and unclear agendas, I've clarified my mission, cut the ties that needed to be cut before I lost all of my self-confidence and moved ahead towards the advancement of my mission. My energy is positive and my work satisfying and meaningful and I am making a difference for those newly diagnosed with breast cancer.

Other lifesavers became apparent to me as I moved my mission of being a breast cancer patient advocate forward. Some came to me through the persistent work of making phone calls and visits to hospitals and breast health clinics and talking, talking, talking about Voices of Hope. Sarah Christensen, former head of cancer patient education at the Mayo Clinic in Rochester, MN became a personal enthusiast of the project. Her efforts on our behalf built many bridges for Voices of Hope in the cancer education community. The Cancer Patient Education Network (CPEN) who in 2013 honored Voices of Hope DVD series with the CPEN Excellence in Education Award, and Join the Journey, a breast cancer support organization, that gives the DVD series to breast cancer patients at the Mayo Clinic along with several doctors and nurses that came to know about the series because of Sarah's efforts.

Some lifesavers just seemed to drop right out of the blue like Tim Braun, former car salesman for Inver Grove Ford & Lincoln where we bought our last several vehicles. My husband was negotiating a deal with management as Tim and I visited. Of course Voices of Hope became a part of the conversation. Again I heard, "I can help you with that!" And help he did finding us Jim Oliver with Aimsmedia Solutions to do the reproduction of the DVDs and design the cover for the series as well as create the Voices of Hope website and a breast cancer support group finder on the internet. Tim also helped out with marketing ideas, funding ideas and general project management pieces. Who knew that buying a new car would lead to a premiere event for the second DVD in the series and many more project friends.

Through listening and learning and trusting that others knew what they were talking about, my life after breast cancer has been enriched beyond my wildest dreams. I have been places and done things that I had no idea would ever be a part of my experience. Thanks to my breast cancer journey my eyes have been opened to the wondrous possibilities this life holds. Numerous are the new friends that have come into my life, some as mentors, lifesavers, medical staff, survivors and friends. All of these people have made a contribution of some sort to my life and have been of help changing the negatives of a breast cancer journey into the positives of another opportunity to get life right after my cancer experience. I've made it. I'm here and happier now than I have ever been thanks to that breast cancer diagnosis so many years behind me now. Whatever your challenge is, I wish the same awakening for you.

Conclusion

"In the book of life, the answers are not in the back."

—Charles Schulz

BY HAVING THE answers in the back of the Book of Life you'd be missing out big time on life's purpose. It is not in the reaching of the goal that we find our determination but rather in the journey that takes us there. Someone cannot just give you the answers, it is the experience of finding the answers for yourself where you truly learn and grow. Hopefully my happenings shared in **Breast Cancer Saved My Life** will be an incentive for you to take a second look at your own experiences to move you toward saving your life as well.

Here are a few take-a-ways that may be of help on your own life-saving journey.

Remember that:

1.   Happiness and joy are the essence of living. You are the creator of that joyfulness. It comes from within you and how you choose to perceive and react to your own experiences.

2.   Faith in a higher being adds dimension to your life, your love and your relationships. Watch for the messengers from your God. They are angels sent to you for help in your times of need.

3. Prayer is having a conversation with your deity, who enables you to build and remain in relationship with him/her and bring you peace, understanding and wisdom.
4. You must watch and be open to love coming to you in your daily living from everywhere in the universe. Again you need to perceive and react to that love and it will bring you happiness.
5. Life is a good and precious gift. Don't waste it as it only happens once for each of us.
6. Gratitude is a powerful attitude. It opens our eyes to the abundance in our lives and a sense of fulfillment while creating the desire to reach out to others and share our love and thanksgiving.
7. Being a gracious receiver is just as important as giving. If we were all givers, who would there be to receive? There is a giving cycle that we all must contribute to. If we don't receive, we cut ourselves from the process and the strengthening of the bond of love doing ourselves harm.
8. Lifesavers come into our life for a purpose. We must listen and trust what they have to share with us within reason of course and then hang on as we see where it takes us.

Thanks for taking this journey with me. I wish you much discovery and joy as you embark on your own life saving exploration.

Breast Cancer Saved My Life

by Diane Davies

Available at:
dianedavies.net
http://amazon.com/author/dianedavies

Chapter 9
Consequences of Decisions Made

After the publication of *Breast Cancer Saved My Life* in the fall of 2015, Diane Davies, author and survivor, began having difficulties with her breast implants from 2004. Chapter 9 - Consequences of Decisions Made tells that story with the honest style and wit that you can always expect from Diane's writing.

THE WISDOM OF 12 YEARS OF SURVIVORSHIP

Chapter 9

Consequences of
Decisions Made

"Choices made, whether bad or good, follow you
forever and affect everyone in their path one way
or another."

—J.E.B. Spredemann, An Unforgivable Secret

I MUST HAVE been about twelve years old when I came home from school with an invitation to a real pajama party complete with teenagers, record player, pizza and late night movies. The party was set for Friday night and I was soooooo excited. My Dad was already home from work and heard me telling Mom about the party. His response was, "Sounds fun. Are you going?" "Well, of course", was my reply!

Dad went on to explain that Saturday was a big day. The house needed to be cleaned and groceries purchased then our family was invited to have dinner at my Uncle and Aunt's home in St. Paul for my cousin's birthday. His question to me was, "So do you think you can go to the party, come home in the morning and help with your chores and then attend the birthday dinner and not be a grouch?"

I made the decision to attend the pajama party and do the rest of Saturday with a smile on my face – not an easy task, as I didn't get much sleep. I was totally exhausted and even fell asleep in the car on the way home from St. Paul that evening. Dad made his point – you live with the consequences of the decisions you make.

In an effort to not be a "no breasted woman", I made the decision back in 2004 at the time of my breast cancer journey, to undergo breast reconstruction. This consisted of having tissue expanders placed under my chest muscles during my double mastectomy. The expander is similar to a water balloon that "expands" the tissue and muscle when filled with saline solution making a pocket in which the implant is placed. This is a process that takes about three months of weekly visits to the plastic surgeon to have more saline solution added to the expander to stretch the pocket "growing" more room for a larger and larger implant. When you reach the size you want to be, you live with it for another three months to make certain the pocket stays which in turn assures that the implant will not move once it is inserted. Quite a rig-a-ma-row wouldn't you say?

So about six months after my initial surgery, I had the expanders removed and the implants put in giving me the new breasts that I desired. Tired of surgeries and doctor visits, I did not have nipples created or areoles tattooed, as I had no plans to be a topless waitress anytime soon. My silicone breasts allowed me to still look like a woman and especially fit into my clothing like a woman without having to deal with breast prosthesis. I was happy with the consequences of my decision.

Some decisions you make can <u>never</u> be changed and yet the consequences continue. Fast forward from 2004 to 2011 in my breast cancer journey. I began experiencing some itching and swelling of my left **silicone** breast early in the fall. Now the only breasts I have are not real. The skin covering the silicone is real and the fat deposits are real but the breast itself is silicone. It basically stays where it is put, does not droop or sag and certainly does <u>not grow</u>. I didn't give it much thought until once again as in 2004 my left breast appeared larger than the right. Bafflement was my first reaction! It appeared that my breast was growing and yet I knew that it could not be happening. So what was going on?

A few weeks later while having my nails done by my regular manicurist, I explained to her my dilemma of a growing breast that can't possible be growing. Her response was quick and sure, "Don't mess around. Get in and see your doctor. Promise me you'll call yet today and make an appointment." She was absolutely right. What was I doing NOT going to get it checked out? I promised her that I would take her advice and call for an appointment. The question then became whom do I call? Should it be my GP, my surgeon who did the mastectomy or the plastic surgeon? I made my decision and called my plastic surgeon making an appointment for the following week.

The plastic surgeon's office as you will recall from my first book From There to Here; A Breast Cancer Journey, was not one of favorite haunts. I'm not a fan of most thing plastic especially flowers and at that point boobs. However, we do what we have to do. I had spent a lot of time in this office suite back in 2004. My return was a bit like coming home! Visiting with the medical staff that had seen to my needs so many years before was fun and interesting. Even the doctor was happy to see me accept for the fact that I was there with a problem once again.

After the surgeon's initial examination, he explained that he felt the problem was one of three things; 1. An infection around the implant. 2. A broken implant. 3. A rare form of a new breast cancer. He suggested we do a breast MRI to get a look at what was happening and make our decision how to proceed with that added information.

Interesting things those MRIs. Loud banging and clanging, huge fear-provoking piece of equipment, uncomfortable body position for a breast MRI, kind caring technicians, sweating profusely— and yet in just under forty-minutes they had taken a look INSIDE my body without opening a wound anywhere! Amazing to say the least. Almost otherworldly!

I found myself once again in panic mode waiting for the MRI results. What if it is a new rare breast cancer? Its been almost twelve years, why not me with a new diagnosis? It does happen to other women. It sure could happen to me. My mood was a bit scrappy, argumentative, and belligerent. Even I had a hard time getting along with me – my poor family.

The good and bad news came at the next week's appointment with the plastic surgeon. The culprit turned out to be a broken implant (good news???) with the bad news being that it would need to be removed – another surgery. I was totally relieved not to have to face #3. My decision came easily, "Let's take both implants out and not replace either one. I was now going to be that "no breasted woman" that I wanted no part of eleven years back.

Breast implants are not a forever thing for anyone. The plastic surgeon explained that to me way back in 2004. Implants have a life of about ten to fifteen years. When you begin to have trouble with them is a sure sign and generally the only sign that they need to be replaced. Like everything else, they get old. Even young women having breast augmentation with silicone implants will be faced with this dilemma at some point down the road.

On November 11, 2015, I went into surgery to have the implants taken out and not replaced. After a few days when the bandages were first removed my initial reaction was WTF! (I never use that word.) I was shocked NOT to see the flat chest I had imagined. I never gave a thought to the chest muscles that had been expanded to hold the implants! Of course they were still there – not very lovely to look at – but still there. I had to remind myself that my chest muscles had been stretched to make the pockets and that of course they would not cut the muscle to give me a flat chest. If they had I would have lost a great deal of movement.

My chest, however, is really quite a mess. The extra boobs of fat are still under each arm, the twist in my left boob from scarring hasn't changed and I appear to have a few bubbles of fat here and there among the scars that didn't show up before. But hey – I don't really have to look at it now do I? For the most part it is covered by clothing and only sees the light of day when I'm getting in or out of the shower and/or when I'm dressing! Truly on the bright side, because of some fat deposits and a little fluid that continues to collect along with those left over pockets for implants, I still have a little cleavage to claim as my own, odd but true. I was joking with my doctor about moving to Mexico to become a drug mule. "All they'd have to do is fill my chest pockets with drugs, sew me up and send me across the border." His quick reply, "The only problem with that is they usually kill the mule to remove the drugs." Probably not one of my better ideas!

The decision to remove both implants turned out to be quite timely. The broken implant on the left was leaking silicone, which had started to travel up my chest toward my shoulder – thus the swelling and irritation. The right implant was becoming sticky on the outside and would have broken very soon. My chest area inside around that implant was already red with irritation. It would have been just a matter of time before I would have begun having trouble on that side as well.

In my mind, this surgery was to be a piece of cake. In and out the same day. Ready to go in a week or so. No problem. Well that didn't happen quite that easily. With an eleven-year-older body, the healing didn't come quite so fast. It took me three days just to wake up from the surgery and when I did I found myself crawling back in bed pretty often. I rather plowed my way through the holidays starting with Thanksgiving doing only the minimum of what was necessary. My new scars are now once again mended and are beginning to fade. They will never be gone completely but that's okay. I continue to LIVE with the consequences of that decision made back in 2004. Some of the results are good and some are not so good. The best part, however, is that I'm still here!

On Facebook recently someone had posted this quote from Josh Shipp:

> You either get bitter or you get better. It's that simple. You either take what's been dealt to you and allow it to make you a better person, or you allow it to tear you down. The choice does not belong to fate. It belongs to you.

Why Kids Need to Know About Mom's Breast Cancer Diagnosis

By Diane Davies author of
Jeannie Ann's Grandma Has Breast Cancer

"YOU HAVE BREAST cancer." Hearing my doctor say those four words in connection with my body was devastating to say the least. Let's try overwhelming, shocking, shattering, damaging, or even ravaging. None of those words come close to describing how I felt when I received that diagnosis. With my husband and adult daughter by my side, the consultation continued. I never heard a word of what was said as I was planning my funeral!

Here I am, however, fifteen years a survivor and breast cancer patient advocate trying to make the journey less lonely and less scary for those that come after me. My intent in writing Jeannie Ann's story was to create a tool for families facing a breast cancer journey to use when they needed to start the conversation where children would be told about the loved one's diagnosis. Reading Jeannie Ann's story will serve as a stepping stone to creating an atmosphere where truth will be told and questions answered.

"Wait! I don't want my children to know that I have cancer. I want to protect them from the harsh realities of life. I don't want anybody to know. I want to keep this diagnosis a secret. I especially don't want to feel or appear weak, or scared and I certainly don't want to cry and really scare my kids."

I get it. I do understand. I've been there. My husband's first wife lost her life in an accident. When we married and had our daughter we never even thought to tell her about this tragedy as she grew older. Great Grandma passed away and the minister leading her funeral was a member of the family. He was talking about this wonderful 101 year old little woman and all of the changes she had witnessed in her century of living. He mentioned the accident among other family trials and incidents that Great Grandma lived through. My twelve year old daughter was distraught and shattered. She explained to us that she felt abandoned by her family and alone. We had lied to her by never telling her. My husband along with his mother and I spent many hours helping her understand the terrible oversight. Children need to know they belong and that they are important enough to know the whole story, good and bad, that we share together as a family. We learned that one the hard way.

So let's focus on this "WHY" it is important that children know about a loved one's diagnosis. First of all children are very perceptive. They thrive on routine because it makes them feel safe knowing what is coming. Any break in routine no matter how small is upsetting for them. In Jeannie Ann's story, the break in routine comes when she gets home from school, a longer tighter hug from mom, no snack and baby brother still in his pajamas from the night before, is her tip off that something is not right. Dinner is a quiet affair – another hint. Anything out of the ordinary takes the safe out of the routine.

As hard as the truth may be, children imagine it worse. Jeannie Ann overhears Mom and Dad whispering after she leaves the table. She hangs around the doorway and hears the word C A N C E R! Now her imagination goes wild. Who has cancer? Is it me? My baby brother? Mom or Dad? What will happen to me? Who will take care of me? With the lack of information, children fill in the blanks themselves often in scary, unhealthy ways totally missing what is really happening.

Keeping cancer a secret can make the child feel shut out and abandoned as we learned with our daughter. Jeannie Ann even imagined that she was the cause of the cancer and the pain because of something she'd forgotten to do or perhaps because of bad behavior that she did do. The illness came as a punishment. This kind of thinking is not unusual and becomes another stress in the dynamic of the family causing a closing of the lines of communication. When trying to keep a secret, the child may hear about the diagnosis from a well-meaning neighbor or even other kids on the bus destroying the trust that the child has in the parent. This can lead to the child thinking that her/his family doesn't even love them enough to let her/him in on the secret.

As hard as we as parents try, it is impossible to shield our children from the stressful parts of life. If we were successful, I'm not sure that would be a good thing anyway. Our job as parents is to teach children how to manage such challenges in life by modeling for them what works for us.

Being honest and truthful with children is important during the good times as well as the bad. When a child thinks the parent is not being truthful, it becomes difficult for them to know when they are being told the truth. The effects of treatment, loss of hair, exhaustion, nausea, sleeping all the time, can be terrifying for children without knowing the facts behind what is happening. Talking about feelings make feelings less overwhelming, upsetting and scary even for adults.

Your child depends on you. A cancer journey can be a loving growing opportunity for the family. It takes work and planning at a most difficult time, however. By letting our children in, we as parents are allowing them to learn how to care and provide support and comfort for others and for ourselves. This is an important life lesson.

Here is something to think about. KidsGrief.ca talks about the Four C's of Child Concern When Someone They Love is Diagnosed With Cancer.

1. Did I CAUSE it?
2. Can I CATCH it?
3. Can I CURE it?
4. Who will take CARE of me?

Keep these four questions in mind as you plan the conversation with your children regarding the diagnosis of a loved one with cancer.

Choose a time when you can focus all of your attention on the conversation. Make it a quiet time with as few distractions as possible. Turn off all radios, TVs, cell phones, and other devices to make for less interruptions. Plan for the time to be a long enough so all questions can be answered. The best place to hold this conversation is at home where all involved are comfortable and feel safe. If at all possible, the loved one with the diagnosis should be the leader with all members of the immediate family in attendance even the very young. Add others only if they increase the child's comfort. People outside the family could possibly add more stress for everyone. I'd be real deliberate about who should be there and why.

If you are the patient, practice saying out loud "I have cancer." That is a tough one. For me once I gave voice to it, it became reality. I highly suggest practicing it so you are able to control your own response. It's okay to cry. You should be honest with those you love and crying is an honest response. Remember there is no age limit for the need to cry. Allowing emotions to be expressed honestly help the children to feel safe and secure.

Be prepared with all of the facts as you never know what questions will be asked. It is important to share what part of the body is affected and simple details regarding the treatment plan. Listen carefully to what the child is asking. There is no need to talk beyond what is being asked or to go into details that may just add to the fear.

Being honest and hopeful is the best approach. If a question is asked that you do not know the answer to, assure them that you'll find the answer and share it at that time.

"Will you die?" is sure to be one of the anxieties on everyone's mind so spend some time thinking about how you will answer that one. Dying is always a possibility so be careful not to make a promise that is actually beyond your control.

Be sure the children understand that they are not responsible in any way for Mom having breast cancer. They did not cause the cancer by their actions or inactions. And just as important, they cannot "catch" cancer – it is not contagious.

"Who will take care of me?" is certainly a topic not to skip over with children. Where will I be while you are sick or in the hospital? Where will I eat? Where will I sleep? If possible, allow the children to have a voice in this plan. Be sure to reassure that no matter what happens, the child will be cared for and that you will try to keep their life as normal as possible under the new circumstances. At the same time, modal for them that it is okay to laugh and be happy during this time of illness.

Children can share in the experience with you by assigning them tasks to help with according to their age level. Teens of course can take on more responsibility but still need to have their own time and space if possible.

Here is a reminder list for parents for after the conversation and as the journey continues:

- Make time for continued conversations with the children and the teens.
- Put time on the calendar for each child.
- Encourage the children to do his/her everyday things
- Check in with the child on an ongoing basis
- Include child in a clinic/treatment visit if possible
- It is okay to say "I don't know!"

- Telling children that a dying patient "is going to sleep" can make bedtime confusing and frightening. Your own beliefs will guide you in this matter.
- If the child seems withdrawn, has an ongoing behavior change or prolonged disinterest normal activities – seek professional help. Your health care team will have suggestions for you as to who to see. Don't let this slip through the cracks. Alert the child's daycare/school to help watch for signs of needing help.

Listening to your child is the most important advice when a loved one is diagnosed with any cancer. Listening is a vast part of communication and good communication helps everyone in the family cope with the changes that lie ahead. Talking with your children honestly and helping them express their emotions will help them feel safe and secure and continue to build trust in you as the parent. Honest communication with your children throughout the cancer journey is of utmost importance. Don't go it alone – reach out! There is plenty of help for those of you who are strong enough to ask for it.

Diane Davies
dianedavies.com
dianedavies48@yahoo.com

www.ingramcontent.com/pod-product-compliance
Lightning Source LLC
Chambersburg PA
CBHW021609120626
46545CB00001B/148